D0098524

THE **SALES ACCELERATION** FORMULA

THE **SALES ACCELERATION FORMULA**

Using **Data, Technology,** and **Inbound Selling** to go from **$0 to $100 Million**

MARK ROBERGE

WILEY

Published by John Wiley & Sons, Inc., Hoboken, New Jersey.
Published simultaneously in Canada.

For general information about our other products and services, please contact our Customer Care Department within the United States at (800) 762-2974, outside the United States at (317) 572-3993 or fax (317) 572-4002.

Wiley publishes in a variety of print and electronic formats and by print-on-demand. Some material included with standard print versions of this book may not be included in e-books or in print-on-demand. If this book refers to media such as a CD or DVD that is not included in the version you purchased, you may download this material at http://booksupport.wiley.com. For more information about Wiley products, visit www.wiley.com.

Library of Congress Cataloging-in-Publication Data:

Roberge, Mark.
   The sales acceleration formula : using data, technology, and inbound selling to go from $0 to $100 million / Mark Roberge.
       pages cm
   Includes index.
       ISBN 978-1-119-04707-0 (hardback); ISBN 978-1-119-04717-9 (ebk);
ISBN 978-1-119-04701-8 (ebk)
1.   Sales management. 2.   Selling.   I. Title.
   HF5438.4.R58 2015
   658.8'1–dc23

                                                2014039741

Printed in the United States of America

10   9   8   7   6   5   4   3   2   1

Contents

Foreword

Sales doesn't get any exemption from the curse of living in interesting times. Everyone recognizes that today we face unprecedented challenges: the consequences of the Internet and e-commerce, the increasing power and sophistication of purchasing, the effects of globalization. There's no shortage of "interesting" challenges confronting sales organizations, sales managers, and their salespeople.

Now stir another nasty difficulty into the mix. Sales is suddenly in the strategic spotlight. Boardrooms across the world are looking more closely at sales strategy than ever before. What's driving this new interest? There are several reasons, but two factors stand out above the others. The first is the huge increase in competition. Today no niche is safe. There's an oft-quoted figure that the average company today has twice as many competitors as it had five years ago. Nobody knows how true this is, but many experts—myself included—believe it to be so. Assuming the figure is valid, that's another way to say that, statistically, the average company's market share has been cut in half. The second factor is the precariousness of the strategy that most companies have relied on to counter the effects of hypercompetition. Ask the average company to tell you its primary strategy for success in a competitive world. I did just that recently at a meeting of corporate strategists. More than 70 percent responded that their strategy was "innovation." And, in response to my follow-up question, "Is it working?" more than half said that it was not.

Now I don't want to knock innovation. It's a fine strategy if you can pull it off, and every company is forced to continuously innovate or risk going out of business. It's just that the knee-jerk response to competition has been to innovate, and, as many organizations have found, innovation has its downside. For one thing, it's a very hard strategy to sustain. Even Apple, the poster child of strategic innovation, may not be able to pull it off for much longer. But there's another less recognized downside, and that's the diminishing window of opportunity. The whole idea of innovation is that it gives you a competitive breathing space—a period when you have something unique and special that puts you ahead of competitors. In the good old days, a decent innovation could look forward to a year or two of advantage in the marketplace before the competition could catch up. Not so today: you're lucky if you have a couple of months at the most. As a result, many companies are questioning their reliance on innovation as a growth strategy.

It's for this reason that an increasing number of leading companies have a new mantra—organic growth. As Jeffrey Immelt of GE describes it, organic growth is "using our sales and marketing assets to take the best business from competitors." There's little doubt that organic growth is a sound strategy. The trick is how to pull it off. The prerequisite is having an excellent sales force that is capable of out-selling the competition. Few companies have any understanding of how to create, train, manage, and grow such a sales force.

Fortunately, there's now no shortage of good advice. The last few years have seen a blossoming of really excellent sales books on subjects ranging from recruiting and training to compensation and sales management. The pieces of the jigsaw are becoming better defined all the time. Yet, to my mind, there's still something missing. However well we might understand each individual piece of the puzzle, we get nowhere unless we can assemble them into a coherent whole.

It's here that Mark Roberge and *The Sales Acceleration Formula* come in. Mark is an MIT-trained engineer who joined a three-person start-up called HubSpot. Let me spend a moment relishing Mark's lack of qualification for the job, which was to build "scalable, predictable revenue growth" or, in other words, sales. First, he knew absolutely nothing about sales and selling. Perhaps that's not such a crippling disadvantage, as it freed him from many of the superstitions, mal-practices, and bad habits that weigh down many long-time sales leaders. But, for sure, if HubSpot had been a larger company, it would have thought twice before offering him a sales job, let alone putting him in charge of sales.

Mark's second disadvantage was his engineering background. There are not many people who can go from writing code one day to growing a sales organization the next. There's a deep mutual prejudice between engineering and sales. The engineer's stereotype of sales is that selling is the irrational art of manipulating people into buying things they don't need using unethical techniques that border on lying, cheating, and stealing. It's for this reason that some engineers, who I think would make outstanding salespeople, would rather starve than take up a sales career. Equally, sales has its prejudices about engineers. Too often, they view engineers as unimaginative, insensitive creatures from another planet. According to this stereotype, engineers are oblivious to people and they take a perverse delight in sabotaging the sales effort. I remember, years ago in Motorola, how salespeople called engineers "the truth-blurters" and did everything possible to keep them away from their customers.

These are dangerous stereotypes and unfortunately their remnants persist even today. The reality is that sales has been forced to grow up in recent years. You cannot succeed in today's B2B sales world unless you embody many of the disciplines that are part of good engineering training: numeracy, logic, and analytical ability, for example. If ever there was a good case study of why these traditional engineering methods are crucial to growing a sales organization, you'll find it here in this book. Mark brought with him to HubSpot the engineer's way of thinking. He analyzed the success factors, set up logical processes, and incorporated measurement and analytics. Throughout the book, what comes through to me is a smart thinker, using his training to pinpoint crucial issues, to think about them in a fresh way, and to come up with workable solutions to problems where others might have given up.

The result has been a sales organization that within seven years grew from the proverbial three-person-in-a-garage operation into a successful $100 million company. The how-to-do-it journey that Mark Roberge describes here is unique in several respects. First, it is an outstanding example not only of how to identify the key pieces of the jigsaw (he has four that are particularly crucial for success) but also of how to assemble the pieces into a coherent and effective whole. Second, as we've already seen, it's the best case I know of how a thoughtful, analytical approach pays off in terms of sales growth. Third, his story covers the whole spectrum of sales growth. It begins with the issues of a typical start-up, such as how to hire your first salesperson, and continues all the way through to the very different set of issues that a $100 million company faces. This is soup-to-nuts with a vengeance and it makes for fascinating reading. Whether your sales force is a tiny one-person start-up or a sophisticated 500-person operation, you'll find much in these pages that is relevant, useful, and thoughtful.

Neil Rackham

Acknowledgments

The chapters within this book unfolded from the inspiration, mentorship, and support from the following people. The only credit I can take is listening to their wisdom.

Thanks to Brian Halligan and Dharmesh Shah for providing me the opportunity at HubSpot and for pushing me to constantly think beyond the norm.

Thanks to my first lieutenants: Peter Caputa, Jeetu Mahtani, Dan Tyre, Heidi Carlson, Andrew Quinn, Brian Thorne, Phil Harrell, Leslie Mitchell, and Joe Sharron. My leadership mission was to find people better than me, hire them, and learn from them every day. Thanks for making that mission a reality.

Thanks to our CMO and my "SMarketing" partner, Mike Volpe. The demand generation innovations executed by Mike and his team were the main driver behind our accelerated revenue success.

Thanks to my mentors and coaches, John McMahon, David Skok, and Ric Jonas, for helping me through the most challenging times of this journey.

Thanks to Will Morel for helping me bring the words in this book to life.

Thanks to Jill Konrath, Neil Rackham, Dave Kerpen, and David Meerman Scott for inspiring me to write this book and advising me through the process.

Thanks to my parents for supporting me with their wisdom in sales and in life.

Thanks to my grandparents, who taught me at a young age that the opportunity to pursue a great education and one's personal passions was not always an option for past generations. I vowed to make them proud and never take these opportunities for granted.

Finally, thanks to my wife, Robin, and my two boys, Kai and Zane, for providing the love, purpose, and motivation that drive me every day.

Introduction

"Scalable, predictable revenue growth."

I jotted these four words down on a notepad. It was 11 p.m. on a Thursday night. I had just signed the paperwork to join a three-person marketing software start-up called HubSpot. I had met the cofounders, Dharmesh Shah and Brian Halligan, while we were students together at MIT. They were smart guys with a big mission: help companies transform their marketing from outbound to inbound.

My job was to build the sales team.

I was up late that night thinking about the road ahead and the mission I had chosen to accept.

"Scalable, predictable revenue growth."

That's what I had to engineer.

Seven years later, HubSpot crossed the $100M run-rate revenue mark. During my tenure as SVP of global sales and services, I led the company to the acquisition of its first 10,000 customers across over 60 countries. I had a team of over 450 employees across the sales, services, account management, and support organizations. Few sales leaders have completed this journey end-to-end. In my case, I completed it without any prior experience building a sales team. As a matter of fact, I had never even worked in sales. I am an MIT graduate. I am an engineer by training. I started my career writing code. Somehow, I found myself in the sales leader seat. Throughout the journey, I challenged many conventional notions of sales management by utilizing the metrics-driven, process-oriented lens through which I'd been trained to see the world.

When people heard about my journey, they became intrigued. They were curious as to how an engineering methodology had successfully scaled a sales team. Their curiosity translated to thousands of phone calls from sales executives and business owners. It led to hundreds of speaking engagements. Eventually, it led to this book. That was not my intent. I was simply trying to provide for my family and contribute to the mission that Brian and Dharmesh had set out to achieve. All that said, I am happy to share my stories of scaling the team. I hope it helps many of you do the same.

I picked up the notepad again and continued writing:

1. "Hire the same successful salesperson every time." (*The Sales Hiring Formula*)
2. "Train every salesperson in the same way." (*The Sales Training Formula*)
3. "Hold our salespeople accountable to the same sales process." (*The Sales Management Formula*)
4. "Provide our salespeople with the same quality and quantity of leads every month." (*The Demand Generation Formula*)

These four components represented my formula for sales acceleration. If I could execute on these four elements, I believed I would achieve my mission of "scalable, predictable revenue growth." For each of these components, I devised a repeatable process, leaned into metrics, and ran calculations, making each of these tactics formulaic in nature. In this book, I refer to these predictable frameworks as the Sales Hiring Formula, the Sales Training Formula, the Sales Management Formula, and the Demand Generation Formula. These formulae reflect the majority of my journey and make up the majority of this book. To clarify, these formulae are not algebraic in nature (e.g.,

"X + Y = Z"). I wish that scaling sales was that simple! Instead, by using the word "formulae," I'm referring to the collection of repeatable processes, metrics, and calculations I used to complete my mission of generating predictable scale.

In Part I, I outline the Sales Hiring Formula. You will learn how to leverage metrics to predictably hire the same successful salesperson profile every time. You will learn that there is no universal mold for "the ideal sales hire." The ideal sales hire depends on the company's buyer context. A top performer at one company may fail at another. However, the process to engineer the ideal hiring formula is the same for every company. Devising this formula early on in a company's development is critical to ensuring that the team hires only salespeople who have the highest probability of becoming top performers. As a practical example, I share the traits that were consistent across HubSpot's top sales performers, explain how I came to this conclusion, and describe how I consistently evaluated candidates on each trait.

In Part II, I outline the Sales Training Formula. You will learn why the "ride-along" training strategy, in which a new hire shadows a top performer for a month, is dangerous. I outline how to bring scale to your sales training efforts by defining the three foundational elements: the buyer journey, the sales process, and the qualifying matrix. I outline how to bring predictability to the training program using exams and certifications. I also provide a blueprint on how to manufacture helpful salespeople with whom your prospects will actually want to interact. In today's buyer-empowered marketplace, a sales team known for its customer-focused qualities will outperform its more inwardly focused competitors.

In Part III, I outline the Sales Management Formula. I wish I could retitle all of my sales managers, calling them "sales coaches" instead. In my opinion, effective sales coaching is the biggest driver of sales productivity. All sales managers should maximize the time they invest in coaching. A common pitfall for new sales managers is the tendency to overwhelm their salespeople, especially new hires, with an endless list of feedback on current sales processes. My most effective sales managers avoided this trap of feedback bombardment. Instead, they perpetually identified the one skill that, if improved, would lead to the most substantial improvement in each salesperson's perform-ance. They then customized coaching plans to hone in on the development of those particular skills. I encouraged HubSpot sales managers to use metrics to diagnose each salesperson's most deficient skill area. I call this sales management approach "Metrics-Driven Sales Coaching" and have keynoted on the topic at many events. I'll explain how to set up a culture of metrics-driven sales coaching, diagnose skill deficiencies through metrics, and motivate desired behaviors through contests and compensation structures.

In Part IV, I outline the Demand Generation Formula. The Internet has completely transformed the way buyers research products and services. Today's buyers are empowered to find the products they want, when they want them, with near-perfect information on the competitive landscape. Buyers may conduct a simple search in Google. Buyers may engage in a social media discussion. The buyer is in control. At HubSpot, we recognized this shift and completely reinvented the Demand Generation Formula to accommodate it. In Part IV, I illustrate how HubSpot built a modern Demand Generation Formula that aligns with today's buyer behavior and generated over 50,000 new inbound leads per month. You will also learn how we took a quantified approach toward aligning sales and marketing, using our Sales and Marketing Service Level Agreement.

In Part V, I discuss technology and experimentation. Over the past few decades, the business world has experienced so many advance-ments in the way Finance manages its budget, HR manages its people, IT manages its data, and sales executives manage forecasting. How-ever, how has technology helped the frontline salesperson? It hasn't. Salespeople have largely been ignored by decades of technological advancements. In fact, in some cases, technologies used to run sales teams actually slow salespeople down. At HubSpot, we worked hard to equip our salespeople with technology to help them sell better, faster. This technology enabled better buying experiences for our customers by providing our salespeople with a view into their buyers' context and interests. Our salespeople were able to engage buyers in the most helpful way at the most helpful time. This same technology streamlined the processes salespeople followed every day, eliminating unnecessary administrative work and maximizing selling time.

In Part V, you will also learn the importance of experimentation throughout the sales scaling journey. Through a cadence of theory development, test execution, reflection, and iteration, I used the results of these experiments to constantly evolve our sales process. I will share the best practices behind experimentation by offering specific examples of some of our most successful work.

Business owners, sales executives, and investors are all looking to turn their brilliant ideas into the next $100 million revenue business. Often, the biggest challenge they face is the task of scaling sales. They crave a blueprint for success, but fail to find it. Why? Sales has traditionally been referred to as an "art form," rather than a science. You can't major in "sales" in college. Many people question whether sales can even be taught. Executives and entrepreneurs are often left feeling helpless and hopeless.

The Sales Acceleration Formula completely alters this paradigm. In today's digital world, in which every action is logged and masses of data sit at our fingertips, building a sales team no longer needs to be an art form. There is a process. Sales can be predictable.

A formula does exist.

The Sales Hiring Formula

1

Uncovering the Characteristics of a Successful Salesperson

World-class sales hiring is the most important driver of sales success.

When you are scaling a sales team, the to-do list is endless. Hiring, training, coaching, pipeline reviews, forecasting, enterprise deal support, leadership development, and cross-functional communication are all part of the day-to-day. Dozens of urgent "fires" are blazing around you at all times. Unfortunately, you have only enough water to put out a select few. Choosing the right fires to extinguish might dictate your ultimate success . . . or failure.

This certainly described my situation in 2007 when I joined HubSpot, a marketing software start-up in Cambridge, Massachusetts. I was the fourth person to join the company and the first sales hire. In my first month, I acquired 23 new customers for the business. Clearly, we had identified a need in the market. We were on to something big. It was time to accelerate sales. It was time to scale.

The to-do list required to scale the sales team consumed my mind. I had a vision for what world-class execution would look like across

3

each component of the scaling process. Unfortunately, like any start-up, funds and resources were limited. A world-class effort across all components would have meant a 150-hour workweek. I had the energy for about 80 hours per week, tops. Corners needed to be cut, at least temporarily. If I could be world-class in only one discipline, which should I choose? Which fire should I extinguish first?

The first bet was made: I would attempt to build a world-class sales hiring program.

To this day, I'm glad I prioritized sales hiring excellence. Even if I was world-class at sales training, managing, coaching, and forecasting, it would not be enough to offset a team of mediocre salespeople. On the other hand, a team of top performers will find a way to win under any circumstances.

Unfortunately, the behaviors I observe in company executives are often not aligned with this strategy. These executives pour their daily energy into closing a big account or running an inspirational staff meeting or coaching an underperforming salesperson through a skill deficiency. Sadly, when it comes to recruiting and interviewing for their own sales team, they simply wing it. They fail to invest in the strategies that will predictably yield a team of top performers. Closing that next big customer in order to make the quarter helps win the battle. Finding a top salesperson, one who will bring in hundreds of big customers for years to come, helps win the war.

> *"World-class sales hiring is the most important driver of sales success."*

So what does a world-class sales hiring program look like? What formula will help me identify whether I am sitting across the table from an A+ candidate?

Over the years, I have hired hundreds of salespeople for the HubSpot sales team. I have advised many companies on their own hiring process. After reflecting on these efforts, I found some very bad news.

The ideal sales hiring formula is different for every company.

I am merely speaking from experience. Some of my earliest hires had been top performers in their most recent positions. I recruited them aggressively—lunches, dinners, the full court press. I showed them why I thought we would be the next big company in Boston. I even convinced a few of them to join. These were the top dogs out of hundreds of salespeople! What could possibly go wrong?

Needless to say, some of them did not evolve into our top performers. What happened? Why didn't my plan work?

I realized that every salesperson has her unique strengths. Some are great consultative sellers. Some crush their sales activity goals. Some deliver exceptional presentations. Some are amazing networkers. Some just know how to make their customers feel like family.

Similarly, each company has its own unique sales context. Some firms sell to marketers. Some target IT professionals. Some sales processes are transactional, while others are complex and much more relationship-dependent.

When the unique strengths of the salesperson align with the company's sales context, it is a beautiful thing. When they do not, it becomes an uphill battle.

Unfortunately, some of my first hires wound up in the latter bucket.

For example, some of my earliest hires were high-activity sales-people that knew how to bang the phones day in and day out. They came from companies with highly transactional sales processes. They operated in well-understood markets with well-established value propositions. The sales contexts in which they had operated had been perfect for their high-activity strong suit. Unfortunately, that was not HubSpot's sales context in 2007. Here is what a typical HubSpot sales call sounded like in our first year:

[Sam Salesperson] "Hi, Pete, this is Sam from HubSpot. I noticed you requested more information on our website. What questions did you have?"

[Prospect Pete] "I did? Sorry, I do not remember that. What is HubSpot?"

[Sam Salesperson] "We are an inbound marketing software company."

[Prospect Pete] "What is inbound marketing?"

[Sam Salesperson] "Inbound marketing allows you to attract visitors to your website and turn those visitors into qualified sales leads for your company."

[Prospect Pete] "Hmmm. How does that work?"

And so on . . .

This was an evangelistic sale with a not-yet-obvious value proposition and a not-yet-established company brand. It required tremendous education in the market. Unfortunately, high-activity salespeople coming from an established company with a no-brainer value proposition were not equipped with the skills to succeed in our context, even if they had been the top dog in their last role.

I realized that the characteristics of a top-performing salesperson would be unique to our business. I needed to figure out what kind of salesperson would be ideal for our company. I needed to engineer the ideal sales hiring formula. Fortunately, this engineering process is applicable to any company.

The ideal sales hiring formula is different for every company . . . but the process to engineer the formula is the same.

Here is the process I used.

Step 1: Establish a Theory of the Ideal Sales Characteristics

First, I listed the characteristics I thought would correlate with sales success. For each characteristic, I documented a clear definition. What did I mean by "intelligence"? What did it mean to be "aggressive"? My intention was to score each candidate on a scale of 1 to 10 for each characteristic. Therefore I needed to define what a score of "1" versus a score of "5" versus a score of "10" represented for each characteristic. For each candidate, I summarized the results on an Interview Scorecard.

Step 2: Define an Evaluation Strategy for Each Characteristic

Once I defined the characteristics I was looking for, I needed a plan to evaluate candidates on each characteristic. What behavioral questions could I ask? Would I use role plays? Should there be an exercise for the candidate prior to the interview? How could I leverage reference checks?

> *"The ideal sales hiring formula is different for every company . . . but the process to engineer the formula is the same."*

Step 3: Score Candidates against the Ideal Sales Characteristics

Back in the early days of HubSpot, I simply filled out the Interview Scorecard after each interview. The process was not overly sophisticated. I used Microsoft Excel. (We were a start-up— I needed to be "hacky.") The key to the process was discipline, not sophisticated technology. I documented my findings and learnings as I went, and used them to constantly tweak my approach.

Step 4: Learn and Iterate on the Model while Engineering the Sales Hiring Formula

A few months in, I had a handful of salespeople on board. Many were doing great. A few were progressing more slowly than others. By remaining disciplined to the process described in Step 3, I was in an optimal position to learn from these first hires and begin to understand our ideal hiring criteria. I was ready to engineer my company's sales hiring formula. I simply went back to the Interview Scorecards for the top performers and asked myself the following questions:

- Which characteristics do these top performers have in common? Are these characteristics predictors of success here at HubSpot? Once I identified them, I increased the weight of these characteristics.
- Which characteristics do not seem to matter? Which characteristics do not predict success? I needed to decrease the weight of these characteristics or eliminate them altogether.
- What am I missing? I had to think beyond the scorecard and reflect on these top performers. Was there another consistent, meaningful characteristic to be found among them? If so, I had to add the characteristic to the Interview Scorecard and start rating candidates on it.

I repeated the same process for the salespeople who were progressing more slowly. I adjusted the Interview Scorecard. The sales hiring formula was taking shape.

As you can see, you do not need to be hiring dozens and dozens of salespeople for this process to be valuable. Reflecting on as few as two or three sales hires can be compelling. That said, if you are truly committed to the $100 million journey, it will take more than two or three great sales hires to get there. Investing in efforts to engineer the sales hiring formula early in the journey will reap significant returns as scale accelerates.

Once you start hiring lots of salespeople quickly, things get interesting. This was my favorite part.

After about a year of hiring, I had accumulated enough data points to run a formal regression analysis, correlating the hiring characteristics with post-hire sales success. As a result, much of the subjectivity could be eliminated from the sales hiring formula. Data is your friend, and statistics do not lie.

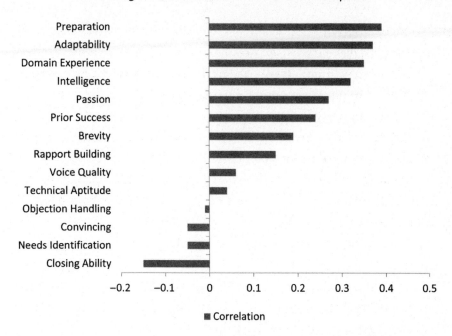

Figure 1.1   Correlation of Sales Characteristics to HubSpot Sales Success (Results of the First Regression Analysis).

Figure 1.1 shows the results of the first model.

Upon first seeing these results, I made an interesting observation: the characteristics that are traditionally associated with salespeople, such as aggression and strong objection handling ability, had the worst correlation with success.

What was happening here?

In my opinion, the Internet's rise in prominence has caused a shift in power from the salesperson to the buyer. My findings were a statistical representation of that phenomenon. With this shift in power, buyers will no longer tolerate being strong-armed into a purchase. They will respond to salespeople who are helpful, smart, and respectful of their needs.

> *"Statistics suggest salespeople who are intelligent and helpful, rather than aggressive and high-pressure, are most successful with today's empowered buyer."*

Statistics suggest salespeople who are intelligent and helpful, rather than aggressive and high-pressure, are most successful with today's empowered buyer.

We were well on our way to developing the ideal hiring formula, customized to our sales context. Every 6 to 12 months, the team reran the regression analysis. This continual analysis allowed us to account for the new data we were collecting as our team expanded. It also enabled us to account for potential shifts in the buyer context caused by product evolution, shifts in buyer preferences, and changes to the competitive landscape. In the next chapter, I will illustrate the hiring formula that resulted after many years of iteration.

Having the ideal hiring formula not only gave me great comfort as we scaled the team, but also served as an exceptional blueprint for future hiring managers. As opposed to driving in the dark, new hiring managers instantly understood exactly which characteristics to look for and how to evaluate each of these traits.

To Recap

- World-class sales hiring is the biggest driver of sales success.
- The ideal sales hiring formula is different for every company, but the process to engineer the formula is the same.
- Statistics suggest salespeople who are intelligent and helpful, rather than aggressive and high-pressure, are most successful with today's empowered buyer.

2

Five Traits Great Salespeople Have and How to Interview for Them

After reading the analysis in Chapter 1, you're probably wondering which characteristics predicted sales success at HubSpot.

Here is the answer.

There were five traits that correlated most significantly with sales success.

1. Coachability
2. Curiosity
3. Prior success
4. Intelligence
5. Work ethic

Figure 2.1 shows the full Interview Scorecard with weights adjusted to the strength of each characteristic correlation.

HubSpot Sales Candidate Assessment

CANDIDATE SUMMARY	
Candidate Name:	John Doe
Date of Interview	1/1/2012
Interviewer:	Mark Roberge
Primary Criteria Score:	71%
Summary of Strengths:	<Insert Strengths>
Summary of Weaknesses:	<Insert Weaknesses>
Next Step Recommendation:	<Insert Recommended Next Steps>

PRIMARY CRITERIA	Score	Weight	Weighted Score	Max Score
Coachability	8	9	72	90
Curiosity	9	9	81	90
Work Ethic	7	8	56	80
Intelligence	6	8	48	80
Prior Success	4	7	28	70
Passion	8	5	40	50
Preparation	8	3	24	30
Adaptability to Change	7	3	21	30
Competitiveness	8	3	24	30
Brevity	6	3	18	30
TOTAL			412	580
				71%

Figure 2.1   HubSpot Sales Candidate Assessment

At this point, I must remind you of one of the lessons from Chapter 1.

The ideal sales hiring formula is different for every company, but the process to engineer the formula is the same.

The foregoing results represent the sales hiring formula for HubSpot's sales context at the time of the analysis. This sales hiring formula is probably not optimized for your company. In fact, it may not be ideal for HubSpot's current stage of evolution. Nonetheless, I have helped many rising companies hire salespeople over the years, especially in the technology space, and I suspect these five characteristics will play an important role in your firm's sales hiring formula.

Therefore, let me share how I evaluated sales candidates for each of these key characteristics.

Coachability

Coachability: the ability to absorb and apply coaching.

Coachability was the most significant influencer of my hiring decision. As I think back to most of the rock stars we hired, their coachability was the personality trait that really stood out in their interviews. Evaluating this characteristic consumed the majority of my interview. Here is the three-step process I employed to evaluate this characteristic.

Step 1: Set Up a Role-Playing Exercise That Models Your Buyer Context

After some rapport-building questions at the outset of the interview, I would verbally set up a role-play with the candidate.

[Hiring Manager] "Jess, let's do a role play. I am going to play the role of VP of marketing at a security software start-up here in Boston. The company has about 20 employees. The marketing team is small—only two people. As the VP of marketing, I ended up as a lead in the CRM system, and I was assigned to you. As you reviewed the lead details, you saw that I had visited the HubSpot website last night and downloaded the company's eBook on inbound marketing. We will role-play your opening call with me. Your goal is to do some light discovery and set an appointment to discuss my needs further. Do you have any questions? If not, please begin when you are ready."

Step 2: Evaluate the Candidate's Ability to Self-Diagnose

Once the role-play was complete, I would ask the candidate to self-assess.

[Hiring Manager] "Great work, Jess. How do you think you did?"

Jess's response to this question represented the first insight about her coachability that I collected. I wanted to see how reflective and analytical the candidate was about her performance. If the candidate simply stated, "I did great," that was a bad sign. I wanted to see the candidate reflect on and analyze her performance. I wanted to hear specifics about what she thought she did well and what she thought she could have improved.

Next, I would build on some of her observations.

[Hiring Manager] "Great reflection, Jess. I agree with many of your points. You mentioned that you could have done a better job handling my question on SEO. If we could rewind to that section of the role-play, what would you do differently?"

A candidate with a high degree of coachability is able to reflect, self-diagnose, and propose improvements to her weak areas. At this point, I would provide the candidate with the opportunity to demonstrate these abilities.

Step 3: Evaluate the Candidate's Ability to Absorb and Apply Coaching

At this point, I would begin some proactive coaching to see how she would absorb and apply the feedback. Absorb and apply: these two actions represent the essence of strong coachability. Some people struggle to even absorb the coaching, perhaps because they are poor listeners or simply don't recognize the importance of feedback. Others absorb the information but struggle to apply it, perhaps because they are less adaptable or less skilled at thinking on their feet. I want to hire candidates who can both absorb and apply coaching.

[Hiring Manager] "Okay, Jess, in every interview I provide one area of positive feedback and one area of improvement."

Both components of this statement are important. If I offer only opportunities for improvement, the candidate might think she is bombing the interview. I run the risk of her freezing up on me, preventing me from evaluating her true abilities. By leading with a bit of positive feedback, I strike a warmer tone. After hearing a bit of praise, the candidate is more likely to feel comfortable and behave normally.

[Hiring Manager] "I thought your opening rapport-building was great, Jess. I liked how you broke the ice and created an immediate connection when you talked about your visit to Wrigley Park as a child. The area in which I would like to see improvement is the depth at which you seek to understand the prospect's goal. Let me teach you how we deepen goal discovery here at HubSpot . . ."

I would then begin to coach the candidate. By this point, I would usually be up on the white board, coaching her and also closely observing the candidate during this process. Is she glassy-eyed or is she taking notes and asking good follow-up questions?

After a few minutes, I would ask if the process made sense. I would request that she redo the role-play, this time attempting to apply some of the coaching I had just provided her.

Now, most people really mess up the second pass. Their heads are spinning. They know the job is on the line. They are sitting with the VP of sales. They've just received my feedback and must immediately apply it. In this situation, I am looking for effort, not perfection.

I will say that I have probably conducted well over 1,000 interviews during my six years in the head of sales seat at HubSpot. Across the full population of candidates I've screened, perhaps only five people absolutely crushed the second role-play attempt. Those who did so became absolute rock stars in our funnel. What's the takeaway? Don't expect perfection, but rather look for effort. If you witness perfection, *hire that candidate at all costs!* You've just spent 10 minutes with a candidate and witnessed meaningful improvement over that short time. Imagine how much progress you could make in a day, a week, a month!

Coachability: the ability to absorb and apply coaching.

Curiosity

Curiosity: the ability to understand a potential customer's context through effective questioning and listening.

I have taught several classes on the subject of sales at MIT, Harvard, and other top universities across the United States. One of my favorite ways to start the class is to ask the students, "What makes a great salesperson great?" The most popular answers are consistent across venues and audiences: "aggressive," "convincing," "great presenter," "money-hungry."

I don't think anyone has ever given me the answer I am looking for. Great salespeople are naturally curious. They ask great questions, listen intently, and probe into points of interest.

Great salespeople ask questions of potential customers in a manner that does not feel interrogative. Instead, potential customers feel like great salespeople are genuinely interested. After all, if the salespeople are truly great, they genuinely take interest in the responses of their prospects.

Great salespeople educate potential customers through the questions they ask. Their questions are thought-provoking and elicit introspection. "You know, nobody has ever asked me that before. Now that I think about it. . . . "

Great salespeople quickly build trust in order to earn the right to ask personal questions and to receive honest answers in return.

Great salespeople seek to understand customer goals, aspirations, fears, and struggles—all through tactical questioning.

Students often ask me, "Mark, how can I prepare myself to be a top performer in sales?" I offer the following advice: the next time you are at a wedding reception, a school networking event, or a party on a Friday night, approach a stranger and ask them questions. See how long you can question that individual without mentioning anything about yourself. If the individual walks away from the conversation feeling interrogated, you need more practice. If the individual walks away thinking, "Wow, that was a really smart and interesting guy," you are on your way to becoming a great salesperson.

So how did we test candidates for curiosity? There are many areas in the interview process, but I will highlight two especially important opportunities.

The first test of curiosity happens the moment I meet a candidate in the lobby.

"Hello, Jess. My name is Mark Roberge. Thanks for coming in today."

Does the candidate start with a question? Does the candidate ask me about my day? Did the candidate research my background and does she take the opportunity to reference an observation from her findings? Based on my responses, does the candidate follow up with smart, open-ended questions to learn more? If all of these things are happening, then this interview has started really well for me (and for her).

The second test of curiosity occurs during the role-play. Let's use the same role-play that I set up in the previous section on coachability.

Ring Ring.

[Marketing Manager] "Hi, this is Mark."

[Candidate] "Hi, Mark. This is Jess at HubSpot. Did I catch you at a bad time?"

[Marketing Manager] "I have one minute."

[Candidate] "Great. I am not sure how much you know about HubSpot. We have an all-in-one marketing platform that helps companies get found online and convert visitors into leads and customers using your website. We have worked with Company X and Y in your industry. I am calling to see if you would be open to a 10-minute call to assess your company's online visibility."

Disaster!

Let's try that again. This time, Jess will be far more curious.

Ring Ring.

[Marketing Manager] "Hi, this is Mark."

[Candidate] "Hi, Mark. This is Jess at HubSpot. Did I catch you at a bad time?"

[Marketing Manager] "I have one minute."

[Candidate] "Great. I noticed you downloaded our eBook about generating leads on Facebook. What specific questions did you have about Facebook marketing?"

Yes!

[Marketing Manager] "Oh, jeez. Um. I was just doing some research. I think I was looking for examples of B2B companies that had seen success using Facebook for business purposes."

[Candidate] "Great. I am happy to share some of those success stories. Have you run any Facebook campaigns yet?"

Yes!

[Marketing Manager] "I have."

[Candidate] "How did they go?"

Yes!

[Marketing Manager] "Okay."

[Candidate] "Okay? What do you mean? "

Yes!

[Marketing Manager] "Well, we did generate a lot of new emails from the campaigns. Unfortunately, I am not sure the people we are attracting are really qualified for our service."

[Candidate] "Interesting. What types of people are qualified for your service? What types of people did the Facebook campaign attract? "

Yes!

Does the candidate lead with great questions? Or does the candidate "show up and throw up," as we say in the industry?

Does the candidate ask about the specific areas the prospect cares about? Or does the candidate bore the prospect with her company's elevator pitch?

Curiosity: the ability to understand a potential customer's context through effective questioning and listening.

Prior Success

Prior success: a history of top performance or remarkable achievement.

Prior success is probably the easiest characteristic to evaluate, especially if the candidate is coming from a reasonably sized sales force. It is the most objectively measurable of the "big five" traits.

[Hiring Manager] "I noticed you were an account executive at your last employer. How many account executives were there at the company?"
[Candidate] "125."
[Hiring Manager] "Where did you rank?"
[Candidate] "Six."
[Hiring Manager] "Wow! Impressive. What metric is that rank based on? Bookings? Attainment?"
[Candidate] "Bookings."
[Hiring Manager] "And the rank is based on last quarter or all of last year?"
[Candidate] "All of last year."
[Hiring Manager] "Very good. And your references will verify that performance?"
[Candidate] "Of course."

I am looking for top 10 percent. If the candidate falls outside of that range, the candidate really needs to rank extremely high on the other key characteristics in order to earn an offer letter from HubSpot.

Evaluating prior success becomes more challenging when the candidate does not come from a reasonably sized sales organization or does not come from sales at all. In these cases, I evaluate prior success through other activities in the candidate's life. How did the candidate perform academically in school? What was her class rank? What were the candidate's standardized test scores? Was the candidate a standout performer on a varsity sports team? Was she the captain of the team? Perhaps she contributed to a major championship? Was the candidate involved in student government or a leader of an extracurricular organization? If the candidate is transitioning from a nonsales background, how did the candidate differentiate herself from her peers in her current/former role? What made her special?

On the HubSpot team, we had an Olympic gold medalist. We had a cello player from the Portland Symphony. We had a former comedian who was featured on Comedy Central. These people pursued their life passions with exceptional vigor and performed at a top percentile level. These people are likely to bring that same passion and competitive drive to their role in sales.

Prior success: a history of top performance or remarkable achievement.

Intelligence

Intelligence: the ability to learn complex concepts quickly and communicate those concepts in an easy-to-understand manner.

Not every sales team needs intelligent salespeople. For example, in a commoditized buyer context, I would bet that work ethic, rather than intelligence, is the superior predictor of success. However, in the HubSpot buyer context, intelligence proved to be a strong predictor of sales success. In retrospect, I believe intelligence was a key trait because our industry was evolving so rapidly. For context, Twitter was a garage project when we first started selling HubSpot. Just seven years later, it is $25 billion technology titan. That should give you a sense of how quickly the industry was transforming in the late 2000s. Our salespeople needed to keep pace as the industry around us took shape. They needed to understand new concepts and communicate to our target customers exactly how those concepts impacted optimal marketing strategies. Because most early-stage companies operate in rapidly evolving industries, I expect that intelligence would be a predictor of sales success in their buyer contexts as well.

I tested intelligence by effectively commencing HubSpot sales training during the interview process. I exposed candidates to new information early in the interview process and observed their ability to absorb the information and communicate it back to me at a later stage in the process. For example, at the end of my first phone screen with a candidate, I would send her training materials on the concepts of inbound marketing, SEO, blogging, and social media. I would ask her to learn the material before our next interview. Then, I would be sure to reference the materials in our next role-playing session.

Here's an example of testing for intelligence and information retention:

[Mark] "Jess, I noticed on your website that you offer SEO services. I always wanted to better understand how I could improve my business's ranking in Google searches. Could you explain how I might go about doing that?"

Her response would offer me a first impression of her performance on this characteristic. To reinforce my earlier point, I am trying to understand two things here: first, how well did she understand the concepts to which I had I exposed her? Second, how well did she communicate those concepts back to me in a simple manner? I would always ask follow-up questions until I eventually stumped the candidate. The deeper I was able get on a topic before her responses suffered, the better it meant she was performing.

Intelligence: the ability to learn complex concepts quickly and communicate those concepts in an easy-to-understand manner.

Work Ethic

Work ethic: proactively pursuing the company mission with a high degree of energy and daily activity.

Work ethic is probably one of the most difficult characteristics to evaluate. These are the three techniques I used to gain insight into each candidate's work ethic:

1. *Observations during the interview process:* A lot can be learned by simply observing a candidate's mannerisms and behaviors during the interview process. This is especially true for assessing work ethic. How quickly did she return phone calls? How quickly did she turn around deliverables (such as her resume, her assessments, or her feedback from the interview)? Did she push the pace of the interview process or were we pushing her? All of these observations provide insights into the candidate's work ethic.

2. *Reference checks:* Conversations with former supervisors or peers represent opportunities to assess the candidate's work ethic. Don't ask, "Did the candidate work hard?" Instead, ask the following questions: "Here are four characteristics that may describe a candidate: coachability, curiosity, intelligence, and work ethic. Could you please rank those characteristics from strongest to weakest for this candidate? Why did you rank these characteristics in the order you did?"

3. *Behavioral questions:* I often used behavioral questioning to explore the level of rigor with which the candidate approached her responsibilities— for example, "Please tell me about your typical work day or work week. What are some of your must-do activities?"

Work ethic: proactively pursuing the company mission with a high degree of energy and daily activity.

To Recap

Every buyer context should have a unique sales hiring formula. For HubSpot's buyer context, there were five criteria that correlated most strongly with sales success. These criteria are probably components of your ideal hiring formula, especially if you are operating in a rapidly evolving market. The five criteria are:

1. Coachability: The ability to absorb and apply coaching.
2. Curiosity: The ability to understand a potential customer's context through effective questioning and listening.
3. Prior success: A history of top performance or remarkable achievement.
4. Intelligence: The ability to learn complex concepts quickly and communicate those concepts in an easy-to-understand manner.
5. Work ethic: Proactively pursuing the company mission with a high degree of energy and daily activity.

3 | Finding Top-Performing Salespeople

Hopefully, you now have some ideas about how to best evaluate candidates for your sales team. I wish I could tell you that is the hardest part of building a high-performing sales team. Unfortunately, it is not.

The hardest part of the hiring process is finding great salespeople to add to your recruiting pipeline. Sourcing great candidates requires tremendous time and effort, but it is a critical element.

Allow me to take you back to September 2007. It was time to scale the team. What did I do? I posted ads across every job board I could find. I received hundreds of applications from a variety of applicants. I probably completed about 50 phone screens and dozens of in-person interviews. I hired zero candidates. Zero!

At that point, I had an important revelation about hiring salespeople. *Great salespeople never have to apply for a job.* Great salespeople never need to pull together a resume. Truly great salespeople have multiple job offers at all times, even if they are not in the job market. Their old bosses are

> *"Great salespeople never need to apply for a job. Finding great salespeople requires a passive recruiting strategy."*

calling them, probably quarterly. "Can I take you to a ball game?" "How is the new gig?" "Are you still happy?" "Are you making money?" "Did they change the compensation plan on you?" "You'll never believe how good things are going over here." "You have an open invitation to be on my team."

Reflecting back on hundreds of sales hires, I can't think of a single person who came to us from a job board or who was actively seeking a new role. Great salespeople are passive candidates, meaning they are not being proactive about changing positions. Shaping a passive recruiting strategy that caters to this demographic is a necessity.

Build a Recruiting Agency within Your Company

But how do you shift to a passive recruiting strategy? Do you simply hire a recruiting firm?

That's what I did at first. I probably worked with about 10 or so recruiting agencies over the course of that first year. Overall, the results were average, though some firms were better than others. At the time, these recruiting agencies charged anywhere between 15 and 20 percent of the base salary of any candidates we hired (a success-based fee). Every firm demanded that I work exclusively with them so that candidates were not contacted by multiple firms for the same job. I ignored that request and always had two or three going at once. If a firm presented a handful of candidates to me and the candidates did not make it through the early stages of the process, I stopped working with that firm and moved on. In an industry with multiple, similar competitors, it's important to be willing to move on quickly if you find yourself unimpressed with the product or service delivery.

In a vacuum, I was able to tolerate the average agency results. What really bothered me was the reliance I had on outside resources for arguably one of the most important drivers of my success. What if HubSpot wanted me to triple the pace of sales hiring? Scaling the external agency model simply wouldn't be predictable enough for me.

I then received the best advice I've ever gotten on candidate sourcing.

Don't hire a recruiting agency. Don't build a corporate recruiting team. Build a recruiting agency within your corporation.

Here is why this was such sage advice: the recruiters at outside recruiting agencies work really hard. They source passive candidates who aren't looking for jobs. They pay their recruiters well, often with performance-based variable packages that incent the staff to crush the phones and fill positions. However, these agency recruiters are not working exclusively for you. When a recruiter finds an amazing salesperson, will they pitch your company first? Will they pitch your company exclusively? Probably not. If the recruiter is a rational, currency-seeking human being, he will prioritize the company that will generate the highest commission for them.

On the flip side, and generically speaking, internal corporate recruiters are very different from the recruiters you find at agencies. They tend to value quality of life, work nine to five, and aren't particularly interested in cold-sourcing candidates. They typically make less than agency recruiters and are paid a base salary with no performance-based commission. Generically speaking, internal recruiters are better at launching job ads, directing inbound resumes to hiring managers, and ushering candidates through the hiring process. In fact, internal recruiters often hire recruiting agencies to do their cold-outreach "dirty work" for them.

The advice I received (and followed) was to obtain the best of both worlds by building a recruiting agency within HubSpot. I went out and found a talented agency recruiter who was thinking about starting her own firm and I said to her, "Why not start the firm within HubSpot?"

"Don't hire a recruiting agency. Don't build a corporate recruiting team. Build a recruiting agency within your corporation."

We paid her and her team as if they were agency recruiters. Instead of a flat base salary, we opted for a lower salary with meaningful performance bonuses that amounted to a higher overall earning potential. Their performance bonuses were based on the fill rates, timing, and long-term success of the hires they made.

The team operated like an outside agency. Most of the candidates were passively sourced. Our guys did a lot of cold outreach and networking. They were prohibited from using outside agencies. The team measured themselves similarly to the ways you would see sales teams measure themselves. How many outbound candidates did they touch this week? How many touches led to connections? How many connections led to a phone screen? How many phone screens led to interviews with HubSpot's hiring managers? How many interviews led to a hire?

Now I had a predictable, scalable process to find great sales talent, complete with internal metrics and ability to iterate on them quickly.

Find Quality Passive Sales Candidates on LinkedIn

Depending on the stage of your business, you may not have the luxury of building a recruiting arm or even hiring an agency right out of the gate. I know I certainly didn't. It was not until my team had grown to 10 salespeople that I was allowed to hire my first recruiter. In short, sourcing the initial team was on my shoulders.

That said, what worked? What are the best techniques for sourcing quality sales candidates?

LinkedIn proved to be an exceptional source of strong passive sales candidates. There are four steps I followed in order to source quality candidates. As of the writing of this book, all four can be accomplished with the free version of LinkedIn.

Step 1: Leverage the Search Capability within LinkedIn to Source a List of Qualified Candidates

Using the advanced search functionality of LinkedIn, I was able to generate a list of qualified candidates to start screening. Here are a few filters I played with that improved search results:

- *Zip code:* This one is pretty obvious. For me, all the hiring occurred in Boston, so filtering by the geographic location of candidates was critical in all searches.
- *Job title:* For the most part, I was looking for people already in sales. Including "sales" or "account executive" in the "Title" field helped me filter results down to candidates already working in the function.
- *School:* Remember "intelligence" was a strong predictor of sales success for me at HubSpot. Screening based on the quality of the undergraduate school helped me limit results to candidates who would likely score high on the intelligence spectrum.
- *Company:* As you hire in your geographic market, you start to identify local companies that have large sales teams with quality training programs.

One of my most effective searches was to look for former employees of companies where I had relationships with the head of sales. Over the years, I have helped and/or networked with many heads of sales, especially in Boston. You might say that many of them "owed me a favor." What I would do is choose one of those heads of sales and conduct a LinkedIn search for salespeople who had worked at her company but had since left. Within 15 minutes, I was able to generate a solid list of people that used to work for her. I would then email this list to her and ask if she recommended any of the candidates as standout performers. Ninety-nine percent of the time, my head of sales contact would be happy to respond with recommendations on who to go after. Often, they would even bring up a few additional names once they were aware of the type of people we were looking for.

Step 2: Screen the Search Results Using the Details in the Candidate's LinkedIn Profile

There was a lot I could learn about a candidate simply from his profile. A brief screen helped me to focus my sourcing efforts on the highest-quality people. The top elements I looked for in candidate profiles were:

- *Indicators of sales excellence.* These include rankings on their team, consistent quota attainment, President's Club attendance, and so forth.
- *Longevity at their current/former employers.* This was especially relevant for candidates at companies I knew had high-performing sales teams. Even a poorly performing salesperson can survive at a company for a year. A mediocre salesperson might survive for two years. However, when I spotted folks that had made it three, four, five, or more years in a high-performing environment, I knew they were likely to be high-value candidates.
- *Alignment between the prospect's current buyer context and our buyer context.* Are they currently selling to large enterprises or SMBs? Are they selling a commodity or a complex product? Is their sales process more relationship-oriented or transactional? These factors help me assess the learning curve for potential candidates. If these aspects do not match my buyer context, that is not a showstopper. I am just looking for some low-hanging fruit.
- *School and major.* As we discussed, "intelligence" and "prior success" were predictors of sales success for me. The quality of their school, the difficulty of their major, and their academic performance were all correlated with these characteristics. To be honest, I think the second-tier schools produce the best candidates. Trust me—I hired plenty of successful salespeople from the MITs and Harvards of the world. Some ended up being top leaders at HubSpot. However, many grew bored within a sales organization and wanted to achieve career progression faster than we could accommodate.

- *Quality of LinkedIn profiles.* To be honest, this had limited impact on my screening process. However, a weak, photo-less profile was a huge red flag for me. With the growing importance of social selling, how can a poor social presence be acceptable? On the other hand, a great profile with a professionally taken photo, 500-plus connections, and loads of recommendations from high-level executives made a really positive impression on me. Again, I would not get carried away here, but any candidate at either end of the profile quality spectrum would influence my impression.

Step 3: Engage with the Prescreened Candidates

Once I found a profile to pursue, I found that being connected to the person through a good friend or fellow employee was an enormous advantage. I would always ask our mutual contact for an introduction, and it almost always got me access to the candidate.

The second-degree connection, while a great resource, is not always available. In the case of a candidate with whom I had no mutual connections, I would guess at the individual's corporate email format and send them a direct email. I never really used the InMail capability in LinkedIn, as I figured his email inbox was more valuable real estate to occupy.

Here is an example of a typical email I would send. In this example, the person I am trying to reach is an employed salesperson at Yahoo! and recent Boston College graduate.

Email Subject: Yahoo!/Boston College

Email Body:

John,

Congrats on all your success! I run the sales team over here at HubSpot. Our current team can't keep up with the inbound lead flow so we are expanding the team. Your background is similar to those of our current top performers. Are there any folks in your network who are in the job market and have a background similar to yours?

Best,

Mark Roberge

SVP of Global Sales

Mobile: 123-456-7890

There are a few reasons why I think this email performs well.

First, the subject line contains the right content. Remember, the point of the subject line is to get the recipient to open the email. In this case, the subject is simple: [Current employer/undergraduate school]. Wouldn't you open an email with that subject?

Second, the email is appropriately brief. At the point of the introduction, I do not need to overwhelm prospective candidates with all of the great things about our product, our culture, or our team. In as few words as possible, I want to encourage these candidates, who are likely not in the job market, to wonder if they are missing out on a life-changing opportunity. Fortunately for me as the author, I believe they are.

Third, the "ask" is not guilt-inducing. I am not going in for the kill. I am asking for a referral. Obviously, I am interested in them for a role at my company, but I'm not going to ask for it outright. By avoiding the hard ask, my approach is perceived as far less confrontational. The recipient feels less "dirty" about responding or helping me. Furthermore, it is genuine. Yes, I am interested in John, but I am equally interested in his friend who has similar successes and is looking for a job.

"Searches on LinkedIn and the 'forced referral' are great sources for quality passive sales talent."

After sending the email, if I do not hear back, I follow up with a phone call the next day. Two nice things about cold-sourcing salespeople: they all have phones (unlike engineers) and they usually pick up inbound calls. It is not extraordinarily hard to get a connection.

Find Quality Passive Sales Candidates through Your Team: The "Forced Referral"

The "forced referral" is a specific tactic used within the context of sourcing LinkedIn candidates, in which a hiring manager leverages the existing network of his team. It was by far the best technique we used to find talent. It is tougher to do when you have only one or two salespeople on staff and you are not growing quickly. Once you start scaling, it works beautifully.

Here is how the forced referral works: I would connect via LinkedIn with all of my salespeople, including my recent hires. About one to two months into the job, once they were comfortable with their new home, I would ask these new hires for referrals. Now, that approach is nothing new. However, it is this specific tactic that worked great. Instead of just saying, "We offer $2,500 for new hire referrals—do you know anyone?" I would say, "I am going to set a 20-minute meeting with you tomorrow. Tonight, I will go through your 275 connections on LinkedIn and look for salespeople in Boston to whom you are connected that look like they may be a good fit for our team." The next day, I show up to the meeting with the 18 people they are connected to that fit the criteria mentioned. They then proceed to tell me which prospective candidates are top performers and whether they are comfortable introducing me.

This tactic is more work up front, but it is beautifully effective.

Understand the Sales Talent Pool in Your Area

The final tactic I used to find great salespeople was to develop a deep understanding of the sales teams in Boston, where we recruited the initial team. How large are the teams? How much does their sales-people make? Are they inside or outside? What is the sales training like? Did they recently change their compensation plan?

As I combed through candidates on LinkedIn, I developed a list of all the companies with inside sales teams in Boston. It was not long before I had interviewed at least one person from each of those teams. In fact, I purposely hit each company. Even if the background of the salesperson looked mediocre, I often took the interview to find out more about the company's sales team.

Here are some examples of questions I asked during these interviews:

1. How much does the company pay their salespeople? How are the compensation plans structured?
2. What is the buyer context like? Is it transactional or complex? Is it enterprise or SMB? Do they mostly have outbound leads or inbound leads?
3. How many reps are at the company? What are the different sales roles? How is the sales team structured?
4. What is the company's sales training like? Do they use a formal sales methodology? Do they invest in outside training or have a full-time staff?
5. Were there any major changes at the company that could cause top performers to consider leaving? Did the commission plan change? Did the leadership change?
6. Who are the top salespeople at the company? For example, you may ask if they are the top salesperson. If they say "no," many salespeople blame the territory. You can ask which territory the best salesperson is in and find a way to network to her. I actually never used this tactic, but I had peers at other companies who used the approach successfully. Apply at your own risk. The point here is to think creatively about gathering valuable information to find top talent.

World-class sales hiring is the biggest lever of sales success. Finding great salespeople is the most difficult part of the hiring process.

> **To Recap our key takeaways in this chapter**
>
> ■ Great salespeople never need to apply for a job. Finding great salespeople requires a passive recruiting strategy.
> ■ Don't hire a recruiting agency. Don't build a corporate recruiting team. Build a recruiting agency within your corporation.
> ■ Searches on LinkedIn and the forced referral are great sources for quality passive sales talent.

4

The Ideal *First* Sales Hire

Thus far, we have covered sourcing, screening, and hiring the initial sales team, but we have not addressed one important question.

Who should be your first sales hire?

I receive this question from start-up CEOs at least once per week. In fact, over the past few years, I heard it so frequently that I devised an informal case, which I teach at Harvard Business School, MIT, and other leading institutions.

Let's walk through this hypothetical case. You need to make your first sales hire, and you have the following four candidates in your late-stage pipeline:

Candidate 1: The SVP of Sales

This candidate used to be the SVP of Global Sales for the Fortune 1000 company you hope to disrupt. He has 25 years of sales experience. In his SVP role at the Fortune 1000 competitor, he ran the entire 500-person sales team and oversaw $2 billion in annual revenue.

Candidate 2: The #1 Salesperson

This candidate worked under the SVP of Sales. He is currently the top salesperson on the 500-person sales team at the Fortune 1000 competitor you're looking to disrupt. He has three years of experience in frontline sales.

Candidate 3: The Entrepreneur

Until recently, this candidate was CEO of her two-year-old start-up, which just ran out of capital. Prior to running her own start-up, she was a salesperson at a large company. The company is known for breeding salespeople with excellent fundamentals, but she has very little sales experience with your target buyer context.

Candidate 4: The Sales Manager

This candidate works at a large company with a large sales team. She was promoted to sales manager six months ago. She earned the promotion because she was a top sales rep and demonstrated exceptional leadership potential to build and develop her own team. She doesn't have much experience selling to your target buyer.

What do you think? Who is your first hire?

Well, of course, there are pros and cons associated with each of the four candidates. I have laid out my perspective below, starting with my least favorite hire and ending with my favorite hire.

The SVP of sales (candidate 1) is my least favorite hire. Nonetheless, start-up founders are typically fixated on finding someone like the SVP of sales for their first sales hire.

Here are the pros of the SVP of sales:

- *Rolodex.* The SVP of sales is likely well connected at the executive level with the types of customers you want to attract. Those connections could be an enormous advantage. In fact, if you have a small addressable market with only a handful of target buyers (e.g., the top 10 telecom companies in the country), the SVP of sales becomes a lot more interesting as an early hire. However, I believe industry connections are overrated in most sales hiring contexts these days. Are there really still a lot of deals being done on golf courses and at ball games? Not really. Strength of network is an easy dimension to screen a candidate on. Many people lean into the characteristic heavily, but for the reasons I mentioned, I believe it is overrated.

- *Industry knowledge.* The SVP of sales likely has great instincts around your buyer context, especially from an executive's strategic perspective. He has great instincts about the optimal go-to-market strategy, sales methodology, value proposition, and so forth that will work for the buyer you are targeting. Similar to his Rolodex, his industry experience is an easy attribute to assess but is overrated in the sales hiring process.

Here are the cons of the SVP of sales:

- *Hesitancy to roll up his sleeves.* I have seen so many start-ups hire someone like the SVP of sales, and upon arriving, his first question is, "Where is my assistant?" The SVP of sales has spent the last decade learning to delegate. Unwinding these instincts and asking him to roll up his sleeves will be no small feat.
- *Lack of recent front line experience.* The SVP of sales probably hasn't directly sold a deal in years, maybe even a decade. Your first hire needs to be out in the trenches, talking directly to potential customers as often as possible.
- *Low pace.* I fear the SVP of sales will struggle to adjust to the high-energy, cut-corners pace required in an early-stage start-up environment.

> *"When faced with the first sales hire decision, many founders put the most weight on senior leadership experience and industry domain knowledge. Don't fall into this trap."*

The #1 salesperson (candidate 2) is a step up from the SVP of sales but is not advisable in my opinion. The only situation in which I like the #1 salesperson is one in which the founder/CEO of the company has a sales management background and is willing to invest the time to properly coach this hire. In this case, the #1 salesperson can succeed.

Here are the pros of the #1 salesperson:

- *Industry knowledge.* Similar to the SVP of sales, the #1 salesperson really knows the buyer you are targeting. The slight difference here is the #1 salesperson's knowledge of the buyer will be much more relevant to the front line. The #1 salesperson will have great instincts around how to connect with the buyer, how to speak the buyer's language, how to find the buyer's current priorities, and so forth.
- *World-class sales fundamentals.* The #1 salesperson is a true sales-man. Anyone who achieves top ranking at a large company can be expected to bring a lot of natural sales abilities, a strong work ethic, and a competitive spirit.

Here are the cons of the #1 salesperson:

- *Ability to succeed in an unstructured environment.* When the #1 salesperson joined his current employer, he sat through weeks of training. He was presented with a pitch deck. He was educated on the sales methodology. He was armed with sales tools to streamline his processes. At a start-up, the first sales hire will need to develop all of these resources from scratch. I am not sure the #1 salesperson is equipped to do so.
- *Lacks leadership experience.* Of the candidates, the #1 salesperson is the only one with no leadership experience. Your ideal first sales hire should lead to many more hires. It would be nice if he had the abilities to both execute the first phase of customer acquisition and build out the initial team.

I like the sales manager (candidate 4). She's not the ideal fit for the role but I like her.

Here are the pros of the sales manager:

- *Willingness to roll up her sleeves.* Unlike the SVP of sales, she was recently selling on the front line and should not have a problem getting her hands dirty again.

- *Leadership experience.* Unlike the #1 salesperson, she has some leadership experience as a relatively new manager. She likely can build out your sales methodology, hire successfully, implement the CRM tools, and evolve into a coach of an eight-plus person team. You should give her the opportunity to prove herself and grow into a sales director or VP. In doing so, you are providing her with a unique opportunity to fast-track her career. Her motivation and dedication to the job will be off the charts.
- *Proven track record.* Her recent promotion was likely driven by her great success as an individual contributor and her potential for strong leadership.

Here are the cons of the sales manager:

- *Industry knowledge.* She has not sold to your buyer. As I mentioned in the assessment for the SVP of sales, I am far less worried about this attribute than most people are. However, unlike the SVP of sales and the #1 salesperson, she will experience a learning curve.
- *Entrepreneurial instinct.* This attribute was also a weakness of the first two candidates, but I want to highlight it here. Entrepreneurial instinct is what really differentiates the entrepreneur from the sales manager. The sales manager will likely ask you, the CEO, about your vision for the company value proposition and the types of buyers you are targeting. She may engage a bunch of these buyers, pitch your vision, and fail to get traction. Since you might not have product/market fit figured out yet, she will be left scratching her head. She needs to learn your target customer's biggest challenges without you having to tell her. She needs to understand how your target customer is thinking about solving these challenges. She needs to take the pulse of your target customer's honest response to your value proposition. After

> *"The most critical value from your first sales hire comes not from the first customers or revenue she generates, but from her ability to accelerate the company toward product/market fit."*

running these calls, she needs the innovative ability to see the patterns, iterate on the target customer, iterate on the value proposition, and accelerate the company toward product/market fit.

The entrepreneur (candidate 3) is my most desirable candidate.

Here are the pros of the entrepreneur:

- *Entrepreneurial instinct.* Of all the candidates on the table, the entrepreneur is most likely to accelerate the company toward the right product/market fit. In fact, this aspect of her role will probably be the element about which she is most passionate. Given how important that piece is, her skills here are tremendously valuable. She will dig in with prospective customers to learn about their challenges, opportunities, perspectives, and priorities. She likely has the entrepreneurial instinct to step back from these conversations and help the CEO and the product team to identify the patterns and understand where to pivot.
- *Sales fundamentals.* I also love that she has received formal sales training and gained experience at a large organization. These fundamentals should enable her to engineer the appropriate sales methodology and structure it for scale.
- *Leadership potential.* Her entrepreneurial experience has likely equipped her with the experience and ability to lead.

Here are the cons of the entrepreneur:

- *Sales management fundamentals.* She has probably never hired or managed a salesperson before. Despite this weakness, I would still bet on her ability to get me through the product/market fit phase of the business. Once that's established, I can monitor her reasonably closely as she begins to hire and develop salespeople.
- *Industry knowledge.* Like the sales manager, she does not have experience with your target buyer and will need to scale the learning curve.

If you are in the process of thinking about your first sales hire, hopefully this exercise helped to frame the decision.

To Recap my perspectives

- When faced with the first sales hire decision, many founders put the most weight on senior leadership experience and industry domain knowledge. Don't fall into this trap.
- The most critical value from your first sales hire comes not from the first customers or revenue she generates, but from her ability to accelerate the company toward product/market fit.

PART II

The Sales Training Formula

5 | Setting Up a Predictable Sales Training Program

Let me tell you a story about a fictional salesperson named Sam and his experience as a new hire at the fictional ACME Company . . . .

It was Sam's first day at ACME Company. Filled with contrasting emotions of nervousness and excitement, he looked up as a tall gentleman walked into the reception area to greet him.

"Welcome to ACME Company, Sam," bellowed Jim, the VP of sales. With slicked-back hair and a stylish new suit, Jim welcomed Sam with a wide smile and firm handshake.

"I am very excited to be here, Jim," Sam chimed back with a nervous quiver to his tone. "I really appreciate the opportunity."

Jim was used to seeing these nerves on the first day. He put his arm around Sam, making an attempt to squeeze out his new hire's first-day jitters. "We have a great few weeks planned for you, Sam. You are going to learn from the best. Remember when I told you about Sue, our #1 salesperson?"

"Of course, how could I forget?" replied Sam.

Jim continued, saying, "Well, that's great news. Over the next few weeks, you are going to shadow Sue. You will observe her calls and ride along on her appointments. Before you know it, you will be on your own, competing with her for the top spot. How does that sound?"

"Remarkable, sir!" exclaimed Sam. "I can't wait to get started!"

Over the next few weeks, Sam diligently shadowed Sue. He listened to her prospecting calls. He dialed in to her discovery discussions. He went on a number of in-person appointments with her. He watched her close customer after customer. It was amazing.

That said, some of Sue's sales tactics surprised Sam. On more than one occasion, she was late to calls and appointments. She did very little research on her prospects' companies. She didn't take an interest in their strategy or priorities. She would show up with her pitch deck and just start talking. Despite these behaviors, prospects loved Sue. Every meeting started with a big smile and a friendly handshake. She connected with her prospects on a personal level, often beginning discussions with banter around kids, vacations, and the performance of local sport teams. Prospects loved her and they bought from her.

Sam was a bit confused by these observations. He thought to himself, "Is selling at ACME Company all about the personal relationship?" Over the years, Sam had succeeded in sales through disciplined meeting preparation and a deep understanding of customer needs. However, Sue, ACME's top salesperson, didn't seem to care about any of that stuff. Sam thought to himself, "Maybe I just need to learn to be a relationship seller?"

This "ride-along" approach to sales training is very common in the industry. However, the approach concerns me, especially as it relates to the conclusions that Sam is drawing from the experience.

My best salespeople are individually great for very different reasons. They each have what I refer to as "superpowers" in a particular aspect of the selling process. These superpowers often differ across top performers. Having a new hire learn exclusively from one of our top performing salespeople would provide a limited view of the ideal sales process. Yes, new hires might get a taste of excellence in one dimension of the sales process, but they would also likely be exposed to some bad habits.

> *"Every top-performing salesperson succeeds in her own unique way. Heavy reliance on ride-alongs during the training process jeopardizes a new hire's ability to shine using her unique strengths."*

This fictitious story is not far from actual scenarios at HubSpot. I had two top-performing salespeople. I'll call them Betty and Bob. Both of them were early additions to the HubSpot sales team and, as of the writing of this book six years later, are still on the front lines doing well. That sort of longevity is no small feat in the fast-paced environment at HubSpot.

Betty and Bob achieved this level of success in very different ways. Betty was the best rapport-builder I had ever seen, much like Sue in my example. She knew everything about her prospects. More often than not, half of a product demonstration with Betty would revolve around catching up on kids or pets or favorite foods or music. Her prospects loved her. They all bought from her. Across the rest of the sales process, Betty ranged from "average" to "very good." Her rapport building is what really set her apart. That was her "superpower."

Now let's take a closer look at Bob. There was nobody better at overall sales activity than Bob. He usually achieved 25 percent more sales calls than anyone else on the team. If you walked by Bob's desk in the middle of the day, you would see 10 tabs open in the CRM. He would be multitasking, gabbing on the phone, and sending an email in perfect harmony. His pace was truly exceptional. Like Betty, his abilities in the rest of the sales process ranged from "average" to "very good." However, his activity volume set him apart. That was his "superpower."

Imagine if Betty had trained Bob or Bob had trained Betty. That would not have gone well.

Bob would have walked away from the experience thinking that succeeding on the job was all about rapport building. Knowing that "schmoozing" wasn't his strength, Bob may have gotten very concerned about his ability to succeed at HubSpot.

Conversely, Betty would have walked away from the experience with the impression that succeeding on the job was all about high activity, thinking, "I'm in trouble, given that high-activity volume is not my strong suit."

I needed a way to expose new hires to the blueprint of best practices for our entire sales cycle. This "best practices blueprint" is often referred to as a "sales methodology." I needed to expose my salespeople to these critical learnings, but also provide them with the flexibility to apply their "superpowers" to the process.

Defining the Three Elements of the Sales Methodology: The Buyer Journey, Sales Process, and Qualifying Matrix

There are three aspects of a well-designed sales methodology: the buyer journey, the sales process, and the qualifying matrix. These three elements represent the "best-practice blueprint" around which a successful training program should be modeled.

"Defining the sales methodology enables the sales training formula to be scalable and predictable. The three elements of the sales methodology are the buyer journey, the sales process, and the qualifying matrix."

The buyer journey represents the general steps through which a company progresses as it purchases a product. For example, many buying journeys start with a buyer discovering a problem that he would like to solve. From there, the buyer may begin educating himself about the problem and the possible solutions available to resolve it. The buyer may eventually create a short list of

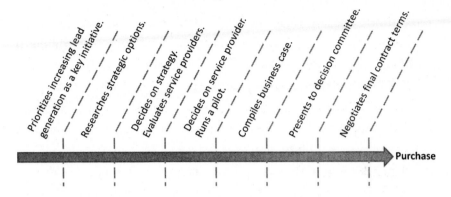

Figure 5.1 An Early Example of the HubSpot Buying Journey

solutions to evaluate. The buyer may pilot one of the solutions. The buyer may assemble an ROI analysis on the cost and benefits of purchasing the solution. All of these steps represent possible stages in the buyer journey.

It is important to start the sales methodology design process with the buyer journey. Starting with the buyer journey increases the likelihood that the buyer's needs will remain front and center during all aspects of the selling process. It also allows the sales team to take a step back and reflect on how the buying journey can be accelerated or streamlined.

An early example of the HubSpot buying journey is outlined in Figure 5.1.

Once the buyer journey is defined, the sales process can be created. The sales process *supports* the customer along his buying journey. For example, if a potential customer requests more information about the company's product, the salesperson should email the relevant information to the requestor. In addition, the salesperson should call the potential customer to find out more about his questions. The exercise of calling and emailing a potential customer is often referred to as "prospecting" and is a common stage in the sales process. A portion of these efforts will lead to a "connect" call with the potential customer, during which the salesperson introduces the company and establishes a bit of rapport with the prospect. If the "connect" call is successful, the potential customer may agree to a follow-up "discovery call" to share more details about his goals and objectives. The discovery call may lead to a "presentation" or "demo" of the solution. Each of these steps represents potential stages in a sales process.

When setting up the sales process stages, it is best if the stages are aligned with the buying journey. Alignment with the buying journey increases the likelihood that the salesperson will be perceived as helpful through the process, as the next steps in the process between the buyer and salesperson are in sync. It is also advantageous if the sales process stages are inspect-able. Inspect-able stages help the salesperson and sales manager understand the true status of each opportunity. For example, "influencer bought in" would be a terrible stage to include in the selling process. It is too subjective. Different salespeople might have different mental definitions of what it means for an opportunity to be at this stage. Furthermore, it would be very difficult for a manager to inspect whether an opportunity is truly at that stage. "Discovery verified" is a much better option. Reaching this stage would mean that the salesperson has emailed the prospective customer a summary of the discovery call and the customer has responded affirmatively. It is very clear to the salesperson whether an opportunity is at this stage. It is very easy for management to inspect whether the opportunity is actually at that stage. The buyer feels aligned with the salesperson through this explicit confirmation of the buyer's goals and solution vision, and should be ready to progress in his journey.

Finally, the qualifying matrix can now be established. The qualifying matrix defines the information needed from a potential buyer in order to understand whether we can help the prospective buyer and whether the buyer wants help. The information is gathered at various stages of the sales process. It is rarely gathered in the same order across different deals.

A very common qualifying matrix that has been used for many decades is BANT. BANT stands for "Budget, Authority, Need, and Timing." Qualification of "budget" means the salesperson has validated with the customer that the value generated by the solution is greater than the cost and that the budget to cover the cost is accessible. Qualification of "authority" means the salesperson has validated the budget criteria with the individual who is in charge of the budget. Qualification of "need" means the salesperson understands the goal the potential buyer is trying to achieve or the problem the potential buyer is trying to solve. A salesperson should be able to quantify the need as well as understand the implications of not achieving the desired outcome. Finally, qualification of "timing" means establishment of a specific calendar time by which the potential customer would like to address the need.

BANT is a bit old–school, but it is a good place to start. As your buyer context evolves and you understand the buyer context more deeply, iterate beyond BANT to a qualifying matrix that works for you. Simply remember to keep the criteria short, simple, and easy to understand.

Create a Training Curriculum around the Sales Methodology

Once the sales methodology is defined, structuring a training curriculum is relatively straightforward. Introduce the elements of the sales methodology in the same order in which you created them. Start with a training session on the buying journey. Dive deeply into examples of the questions buyers are exploring at each stage of the buying journey. Help the new hires get into the buyer's head during each stage of the journey.

Once the buyer journey training is complete, move on to the sales process. Develop a session that introduces the sales process and the qualifying matrix. Then create separate sessions that dive deeply into

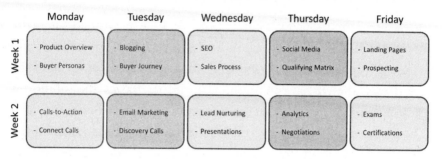

Figure 5.2   Sample Sales Training Curriculum

each stage of the sales process. Have one session on prospecting, another on the connect call, another on the discovery call, and so forth. As the team grows, empower the top salespeople to teach one of these classes, especially if one is suited to their "superpower." This approach is far different from ACME's ride-along strategy. Unlike ACME, you're matching superpowers to specific training topics. You, as the head of sales, have preapproved the content, but you are delegating the work to your top salespeople, who will appreciate the professional development opportunities they are offered.

A sample agenda and course curriculum from the early HubSpot days is shown in Figure 5.2.

Adding Predictability to the Sales Training Formula

I have another major concern with the traditional "ride-along" approach to sales training.

> *A "ride-along" sales training strategy is neither scalable nor predictable.*

What if I had to accelerate sales hiring? How many new hires could possibly shadow each top performer? Are these new hires going to be a distraction to

> "A 'ride-along' sales training strategy is neither scalable nor predictable."

the top performers? How should I quantify the success of the program? How should I audit and improve it?

I needed a sales training system in which success could be measured. I needed a sales training formula that could be iterated in a scientific way.

For this reason, I added an exam and several certifications to the training process. The exam was focused on factual information, such as product knowledge. New hires were subjected to a 100-question exam at the end of training to ensure they left the program with a satisfactory level of product acumen. The exam was a stressful event. New hires crammed for the test as if it were a college final. On some occasions, trainees were let go for a poor performance on the exam. Needless to say, the tests were not taken lightly.

In contrast to the exams, certifications were often used to test qualitative skills, such as the ability to navigate certain stages of the sales process. For example, in order to graduate from training, new hires would need to be certified on the "discovery" stage. They would be provided with a scenario in which a prospective customer had made it to the discovery stage of the sales process, and the trainee would be asked to conduct the discovery call. They would role-play the scenario with one of our sales trainers.

After the role-play, the sales trainer would fill out a certification evaluation specific to the relevant stage. There were specific behaviors we were looking to observe in the "discovery" role-play, such as the new hire's ability to start the conversation with open-ended questions, listen to the prospect and dig deeper into areas of interest, and address the various aspects of our qualifying matrix. The certification rubric clearly defined what each of these behaviors were and what kinds of performances would merit scores of 1, 5,

"Exams and certifications add predictability to the sales training formula. They also provide the platform to learn from and iterate on the formula."

7, or 10. The sales trainer wouldn't just say, "Good job here, bad job here." There was a quantifiable result that came from the certification process. In fairness to the trainees, we would share the certification structure in advance of the exercise so that expectations were clearly established.

It was critical that the evaluator of the role-play, in this case the sales trainer, was not the trainee's hiring manager. Because hiring managers were accountable for the decisions to hire individual trainees, conflicts of interest would arise if the hirers were then asked to grade the hires. Fortunately, the sales trainers didn't have these biases. The sales trainers' responsibility was to make sure that the company understood accurately the performance of each of the new hires coming out of training. By avoiding any conflicts of interest, hiring managers were strongly incented

Discovery Call Certification

SALESPERSON SUMMARY

Salesperson Name:	John Doe
Primary Criteria Score:	80%
Summary of Strengths:	<strength #1>
	<strength #2>
Summary of Improvement Areas:	<improvement area #1>
	<improvement area #2>
Certification Achieved:	Yes

PRIMARY CRITERIA	Score (1 to 10 Scale)	Weight	Weighted Score	Max Score
Preparation for Discovery Call	8	5	40	50
Logistics Setup	9	5	45	50
Energy/Voice Tone	9	6	54	60
Rapport/Commonality	10	5	50	50
Trust Developmet	7	7	49	70
Agenda/Expectations	9	5	45	50
Understanding Buyer Goals	10	10	100	100
Understanding Buyer Plan	6	10	60	100
Understanding Buyer Challenges	6	8	48	80
Understanding Buyer Timeline	9	10	90	100
Understanding Budget/Authority	4	8	32	80
Discovery on Traffic Generation	9	6	54	60
Discovery on Lead Conversion	8	6	48	60
Discovery on Lead Nurturing	9	6	54	60
Discovery on Analytics	8	6	48	60
Challenge/Re-set Strategy	7	10	70	100
Next Steps	10	8	80	80
TOTAL			967	1210
				80%

Figure 5.3   Sample Discovery Call Certification

to engage with new hires early in training and work hard with them to ace the certifications. The new hires' evaluation performance was a reflection not only of their own talent but also of the hiring managers' ability to find and develop talent.

Figure 5.3 shows an example certification for the "discovery" stage of the sales process.

Constant Iteration on the Sales Process

With a well-defined sales methodology, a detailed course agenda, and a strong set of performance exams and certifications in place, I was well on my way to a scalable, predictable sales training formula.

The other advantage of having this structure in place was the establishment of a baseline foundation from which to measure and iterate. The sales training formula needs to be constantly evolving, reacting to changes in the business, just like the sales hiring formula.

Here are a few examples of tools I used to foster iteration on the sales training formula, as well as circumstances that justified iteration.

1. *Six-Month Feedback Forms:* Once a hire was on the job for six months, we asked him to complete a review of the sales training program. I liked the timing of this review because, by this stage, a salesperson had gained some experience on the floor and could reflect on which aspects of training were most and least helpful. My favorite question in this review asked the salesperson to rank the training sessions in order from most to least valuable. I also liked to ask about potential subjects that were missing from the curriculum.

2. *Correlations between Training Performance and Sales Performance:* Just like the analyses we ran in Part One, exploring correlations between hiring characteristics and eventual sales performance, the same set of analyses were conducted to correlate training performance to sales performance. If a new hire achieved a high

score on the product exam, did that predict success in the field? Did a low score predict failure? What about the sales certifications? Did they predict success? If correlations did not exist, we would really need to question whether we had the right sales training formula in place. The strength of the correlations allowed us to iterate on the formula, leaning into the aspects of training that seemed to be influencing sales success. As expected, we found sales training scores to be an even better predictor of success than the sales hiring scores were.

3. *Desired Behavior Changes in the Sales Team:* As the business evolved, whether because of new product developments, new addressable markets, or necessary iterations to the sales model based on observations in the funnel, the existing sales team needed to be retrained and the sales training formula needed to be adjusted. Having a structured sales training formula already in place made it easy for the organization to evaluate where and how to adjust the sales training formula to accommodate the evolution of our business.

To Recap

- Every top-performing salesperson succeeds in her own unique way. Heavy reliance on ride-alongs during the training process jeopardizes a new hire's ability to shine using her unique strengths.
- A "ride-along" sales training strategy is neither scalable nor predictable.
- Defining the sales methodology enables the sales training formula to be scalable and predictable. The three elements of the sales methodology are the buyer journey, the sales process, and the qualifying matrix.
- Exams and certifications add predictability to the sales training formula. They also provide the platform to learn from and iterate on the formula.

6 | Manufacturing Helpful Salespeople Your Buyers Trust

Today's buyers have all the control in the buying/selling process. Buyers can easily go online and find the top vendors in a given space. They can research differences in price and functionality across the various vendors. Buyers can find customers and ex-customers to talk to in social media. Often, buyers can try the product online for free, and sometimes they can even buy the product right there online.

So, why do we even need salespeople? Good question.

In this new buyer/seller paradigm, salespeople must prove their worth by adding more value to the process. Sales is no longer about memorizing the call script, the price book, and the top 10

"Buyers should not be asked to understand the salesperson's solution and how it can help with their own goals. Instead, the salesperson should understand the buyers' goals and how his own solution can help achieve those goals."

objections. It's about being a genuine consultant and trusted advisor to potential customers.

Train Your Salespeople to Experience the Day-to-Day Job of Potential Customers

Salespeople need a high degree of business acumen in order to fully understand their buyers' goals. Salespeople need to transform their product's generic messaging into a customized story that resonates with the buyer, addresses the buyer's needs, and uses the buyer's terminology.

The best-trained salespeople have experienced the day-to-day job of their potential customers.

This modern form of selling requires the salesperson to truly understand what it's like to be in their customer's shoes. What do they do all day? What is easy about the job? What is hard? What causes stress? What do individuals in this role like to do? What do their bosses want them to do? How is success measured?

Once the salesperson truly understands the day-to-day job of the buyer, the salesperson can then effectively relate to the buyer. The salesperson can connect with the buyer, earn the buyer's trust, and appreciate the buyer's unique perspectives. The salesperson can understand where the buyer wants to go because the salesperson has been at both the starting gate and the finish line. The salesperson can advise the buyer. The salesperson can *help* the buyer.

Providing our salespeople with an in-depth understanding of our buyers' day-to-day existence became a key goal of my sales training formula. In the pages that follow, you'll see how I did it.

In the first few years of HubSpot, we targeted marketing professionals. Therefore, my sales training goal was to teach our new sales hires what it was like to be a marketer. New sales hires did not spend their first few weeks in sales training, memorizing scripts and discussing objections. Instead, our new sales hires spent their first few weeks at HubSpot developing their own website, writing their own blog, and creating their own social media presence. By the completion of training, our new sales hires would often rank at the top of Google search results for dozens of keywords. They built social media followings of hundreds of people for their websites. They published blog articles, set up landing pages, ran A/B tests, segmented leads, created email nurturing campaigns, and analyzed the conversion of website visitors to leads to customers, all using the HubSpot software.

Sales hires *felt* the pain of a marketer because they *lived* through it.

By the time new hires made their first prospecting calls, they knew more about inbound marketing, blogging, and social media than 90 percent of the marketers on whom they were calling. They could genuinely understand these marketers. They could genuinely advise them. They could genuinely help them.

The websites and blogs the new hires created did not need to be relevant to HubSpot's business. In fact, I preferred when they were not. I wanted the blogs to cover topics about which my salespeople were passionate. They wrote about chinchillas, the New England Patriots, and secret eateries in Boston. Because the websites represented authentic interests, many salespeople continued to update their websites even after training was over. As our product and industry evolved, salespeople often experimented with the newest features on their own websites first, enabling them to stay one step ahead of the customer on feature fluency.

> *"The best-trained salespeople have experienced the day-to-day job of their potential customers."*

In the early interactions with skeptical buyers, our salespeople would state, "Listen. Most people are skeptical when they hear about inbound marketing for the first time. I was skeptical too. I just joined the company six months ago. Like you, I do not consider myself to be a technical person. I used to sell insurance before coming here. I knew nothing about blogging, SEO, or social media. But this stuff works! Look at this blog I developed in training. It literally took me a few days of effort. Do a Google search for 'best Italian food in Boston.' That is my website right there. The first listing in Google! Now try searching for 'cupcakes in Boston.' There I am again! You can do this. I can help you do this."

Enable Your Salespeople to Build Their Personal Brand with Potential Customers Using Social Media

I'll tell you about one other tactic I used to manufacture a sales team that our buyers loved. Every salesperson has the opportunity to be perceived as a thought leader by his potential buyers. I turned my guys into true thought leaders of digital marketing.

Here is a true story.

The VP of sales from a Fortune 500 company emails me one day. "Mark. We need your help on our marketing strategy. I would like to go to lunch with you and our VP of marketing."

I responded, "Great. Shall I meet you at your office tomorrow at noon?"

"No. We'll come to you," he replied. "Pick your favorite restaurant near your office, and we will meet you there."

So I did.

The next day, the VP of sales and VP of marketing showed up to the lunch with a deck that perfectly framed their problem and proposed solution. They had analyzed the past 12 months of their marketing funnel. They showed me their website traffic growth, their visibility in organic searches, and their conversion rates from visitor to lead to trial to customer. They had theories as to how they compared with the industry, why they may have been struggling in certain areas, and how they could improve.

We worked on the deck for 90 minutes. I shared industry benchmarks of which they were unaware. I confirmed the elements of their strategy I felt were most compelling. I challenged them where I thought they could improve. I told stories about customers that had faced similar challenges and how they had overcome those challenges.

They took diligent notes. By the time lunch had ended, we were all pleased with the agreed-upon strategy. They had a clear under-standing of their achievable goals and a strategy to get there.

The check came. I reached for my wallet. "No, Mark. We have this," interrupted the VP of sales as he brushed aside my hand. "We really appreciate your time."

Shortly thereafter, that Fortune 500 company signed on as a customer. No additional meetings were necessary.

That is modern selling.

Modern selling feels less like a seller/buyer relationship and more like a doctor/patient relationship.

When a doctor asks, "Do you smoke? Does heart disease run in your family?" You do not lie. You see the diploma on the wall and you tell the truth. You know the doctor is there to help you. She is trying to diagnose your issue and fix it. When she diagnoses your condition and prescribes a medication, you don't say, "Let me think about it" or "Can I get 20 percent off?" You take the pills.

> *"Modern selling feels less like a seller/buyer relationship and more like a doctor/patient relationship."*

The VP of sales at the Fortune 500 company trusted me as if I were a doctor. He trusted my diagnosis. He trusted the solution I prescribed. He ultimately succeeded. I helped him.

Now, I did not earn this trusted advisor status simply by being the SVP of sales at HubSpot. I developed this authoritative status by using the Internet to share my views and help others. I frequently shared best practices on Twitter. I retweeted techniques from other thought leaders I respected. I wrote about best practices on the HubSpot blog, in LinkedIn posts, and on other top blogs across the industry. I commented on discussions and articles, always trying to add value to the conversation.

Through these efforts, I developed a following. I developed a reputation as a thought leader in the world of sales and marketing. As of the writing of this book, I receive at least one request a day from new potential buyers seeking my assistance.

Social media presents an opportunity for all salespeople to be perceived as trusted advisors by their buyers. Salespeople should take some time normally spent prospecting and reallocate it to social media participation. The rewards are greater.

You may ask yourself, "Who has time for these efforts?" Make time. Take time away from the initiatives that are working less effectively and reinvest that time in these more modern and effective tactics. If you are a salesperson and you attend a chamber of commerce meeting twice per month, try going only once this month and using the time saved to participate in conversations with your buyers online. If you are a salesperson and you plan to cold-call for 10 hours this week, cold-call for only eight hours and use the time saved to write a blog article about a question your buyers frequently ask you.

As a sales leader, consider encouraging your salespeople to stop investing in the tactics that aren't yielding results and start trying some of these more modern methods of connecting with buyers. Here are some additional tactics with which salespeople can experiment.

> *"Social media presents an opportunity for all salespeople to be perceived as trusted advisors by their buyers. Salespeople should take some time normally spent prospecting and reallocate it to social media participation. The rewards are greater."*

1. Find the people on Twitter that your prospects follow. They may be journalists. They may be thought leaders. They may be executives at companies that complement your offering. Retweet their posts. Many of them will start to follow you. Send them a direct message and introduce yourself. Set up a phone call. Ask how

you can help them. Help them. The next time you publish an article, ask if they would mind promoting the content to their network. Only ask for this favor if you feel your content is relevant to their audience.

2. Find the LinkedIn groups in which your prospects are active. Answer questions in the group. Pose your own questions and engage with those who respond. Include links to topical content your company has available. If no group exists, start one.

3. Find the blogs that your prospects read. Read the blogs for 15 minutes every day. Retweet one or two and promote them in your LinkedIn status. Comment on the blog. Make sure your name on the comment links back to your LinkedIn profile or your company. Bloggers love comments. Good ones will respond to you. Comment back to them. The next time you publish something, ask the blogger to promote it. Build a relationship. Ask if he would like you to submit a guest blog piece.

4. Participate in your company's blog. Check your email's "Sent Items" folder. Often times you find yourself fielding the same questions from multiple prospects. You've found an industry pain point! That makes for excellent blog content. If a question comes up routinely, imagine how many people would be interested in the answer.

To Recap

- Buyers should not be asked to understand the salesperson's solution and how it can help with their own goals. Instead, the salesperson should understand the buyers' goals and how his own solution can help achieve those goals.
- The best-trained salespeople have experienced the day-to-day jobs of their potential customers.
- Modern selling feels less like a seller/buyer relationship and more like a doctor/patient relationship.

- Social media presents an opportunity for all salespeople to be perceived as trusted advisors by their buyers. Salespeople should take some time normally spent prospecting and reallocate it to social media participation. The rewards are greater.

PART III

The Sales Management Formula

7 | Metrics-Driven Sales Coaching

In many ways, a sales manager's title should be "sales coach." Maximizing sales managers' time spent on coaching is one of the most effective levers to drive sales productivity. In scaling HubSpot's sales organization, I was constantly challenged to find new ways to reinforce a culture of sales coaching, knowing it needed to be central to our process. This chapter outlines the approach I used, a methodology I call "metrics-driven sales coaching."

> *"Effective sales coaching by sales managers is the most important lever to drive sales productivity."*

What does effective coaching look like? What does ineffective coaching look like? Let's start with an example. For context, I've been trying to learn the game of golf for the past 15 years, and I've taken many coaching lessons along the way. Some of these lessons have been better than others.

Here's what one of the weaker coaches once told me: "Mark, take a swing. . . . Okay. Now try this grip and lean back a bit. Put more weight in your back foot. Think one o'clock, not two o'clock, on your backswing, and turn your wrists over sooner as you strike the ball."

Whoa, partner! You lost me. Come again?

Another golf pro, who was far more helpful, took a different approach. "Mark, take a swing . . . Okay. Now try this grip. Take 100 swings like that." Twenty minutes later he asked, "How does that feel?"

"Great," I said.

"Okay," he replied. "Now try putting more weight on your back foot. Take another 100 swings like that." Twenty minutes later he asked, "How does that feel?"

"Fantastic," I said.

That is effective sales coaching.

The coach from my first example made a common mistake. Lots of new sales managers err on the side of throwing everything they know at the salespeople they're trying to develop.

> *"A common sales management mistake is to overwhelm the salesperson with coaching too many skills simultaneously. Pick one skill and focus."*

This situation occurs most often when a sales manager receives a new sales hire right out of training. The sales manager will likely see an enormous gap between where the new salesperson is performing and where the sales manager would like him to perform. The sales manager proceeds to overwhelm the salesperson with pages and pages of feedback. I can practically see the salesperson's head spinning. The manager's attempt to simultaneously develop the salesperson across a spectrum of skills results in no skills being developed at all.

The best sales managers, just like the second coach in my golf story, can identify the *one* skill that will have the *biggest* impact on a salesperson's performance, and then customize a coaching plan around developing that skill.

If they're *really* good, sales managers will use metrics to properly diagnose which skill should be prioritized.

Thus, "metrics-driven sales coaching" begins.

Implementing a Coaching Culture throughout the Organization

In the first few months of scaling the sales team from one to eight people, implementing a metrics-driven coaching culture was easy. I was the only leader and I followed my own process. However, as I scaled up to 15+ managers and added additional director- and VP-level layers within the organization, reinforcing my cultural vision was a far bigger challenge.

I've summarized the process I ended up using in Figure 7.1.

On the second afternoon of every month, I would meet with each of my directors—each of whom oversaw a team of roughly 50 salespeople—to inspect their monthly coaching plans.

As we'd walk through their plans for each salesperson, I'd ask them three questions:

1. What skill will you work on this month with this salesperson?
2. How did you decide on that skill?

	First Day of Month	Second Day of Month
Morning	**Salesperson/Manager Independent Reviews** ➤ Reflect on qualitative performance ➤ Review individual metrics ➤ Reflect on Skill Development Plan(s)	**Director Meets with Manager** ➤ Review Skill Development Plans for each salesperson
Afternoon	**Manager Meets with Salesperson** ➤ Discuss qualitative performance ➤ Review individual metrics ➤ Co-Create Skill Development Plan	**VP Meets with Director** ➤ Review Skill Development Plans for each salesperson

Figure 7.1   Process to Hold the Sales Organization Accountable to a Metrics-Driven Sales Coaching Culture

3. What is the customized coaching plan you will use to develop the skill?

In advance of these meetings, all of the sales directors would meet with their managers on the second morning of each month to inspect their coaching plans. The directors would walk through the plans for each salesperson and ask the same questions I was going to ask them later that afternoon. Because of this meeting, the sales managers would sit down on the first afternoon of each month with each of their salespeople, review their metrics, and work together to create a personalized coaching plan for each salesperson. Because of these meetings, each sales manager and salesperson would review their performance metrics on the first morning of every month. The organization was accountable to a monthly cadence of sales coaching preparation.

Creating the Coaching Plan Together with the Salesperson

When the sales manager sits down one-on-one with each salesperson to create a coaching plan on the first day of each month, it's a highly interactive meeting. The manager doesn't say, "John, I reviewed your performance last month. Here's what I saw. Here's what we're going to work on, and here's how we're going to do it." That approach simply does not empower salespeople or create buy-in. That approach squanders the opportunity to use the meeting as a great learning opportunity in which the salesperson can constructively think about his personal development.

By developing plans together with the salesperson, the sales manager empowers her team members to analyze their own results and diagnose their own skill deficiencies through a sequence of questions. Such a sequence of questions, stated from the sales manager's perspective, is listed here.

"Good to see you, John. How do you think you did last month?"

"Qualitatively speaking, what do you think you did well and what do you think you can improve on?"

"Let's review the numbers. Here are the call activity metrics for the entire team. What are your observations about your performance on this chart?"

"Let's move on to the next chart on connect rates. What do you see here?"

A sales manager should continue through all the key metrics. When interesting observations arise, she should dive in a bit, asking, "Why do you think your performance here was so strong (or so weak) relative to your peers in this area of the funnel?"

After running through the metrics, the sales manager should ask the most important (two-part) question:

"So, reflecting on your qualitative observations and the metrics that we ran through, which skill do you think we should work on this month, and what's the best way that I can help you with that skill?"

More often than not, the sales manager will already have a pretty good idea of which skill she wants to work on with the salesperson. However, the sales manager should be willing to adjust her plan based on the salesperson's insightful contributions to the discussion. This flexible approach maximizes the buy-in and empowerment of the salesperson. It teaches salespeople to be their own independent coach, to reflect on their

"Use metrics to diagnose which skill development area will have the biggest impact on a salesperson's performance. Customize the coaching plan to that skill area. Execute 'metrics-driven sales coaching.'"

deficiencies, and to customize coaching plans so they can improve on their own.

I also encouraged the HubSpot sales managers to use the initial monthly meetings to schedule their follow-up coaching sessions.

> "I agree, John. It seems like working on 'developing a sense of urgency' with your early-stage opportunities is a good skill to work on this month. I like your idea of recording two discovery calls that we can sit down together and review. It looks like you and I are both open next Tuesday at 10 a.m. and then the following Thursday at 4 p.m. Let's book those times right now. Please have a recording of a qualifying call prepared for each of these coaching meetings."

My sales managers felt good about this time management strategy. They knew they were prioritizing time to coach salespeople on their biggest needs, rather than constantly reacting to issues as they arose. They were concentrating on the skills that would have the greatest impact on their team's performance. What could possibly be a higher priority than that?

Examples of Metrics-Driven Skill Diagnosis and Coaching Plans

You may be wondering, "Which sales metrics are best to track?"

The answer varies from company to company. That said, as you evaluate your firm's situation, I recommend keeping the first pass relatively simple by starting with the high-level metrics that are already being tracked.

Take a look at the simple model in Figure 7.2. This chart illustrates a basic funnel of leads created, leads worked, demos delivered, and customers closed in the prior month. Each pattern represents a different salesperson on the team. This simple model illustrates where mediocre performers are deviating from top performers and where the largest conversion leakage occurs for each salesperson.

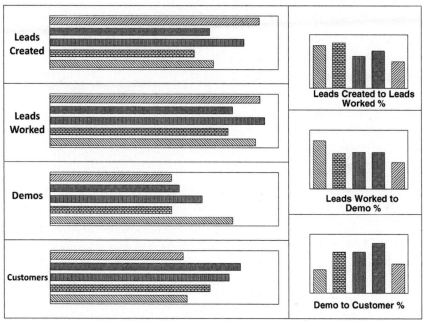

Each pattern represents a different salesperson's performance in a given month

Figure 7.2   Comparing Sales Funnel Activity of Each Member of a Sales Team in a Given Month

Let's look at the salesperson represented by the checkered pattern, listed as the fourth down in the chart. Last month, he worked the fewest leads. Why might that be? Start by asking him directly, in order to get his initial thoughts. Then, offer advice based on your perspective and experience. Here are some possible diagnoses and corresponding coaching plans for this scenario:

1. *Overinvestment in unqualified opportunities:* Maybe this salesperson isn't qualifying opportunities properly at the beginning of the buyer journey, thus investing lots of demo time on opportunities that are unlikely to close. This diagnosis would be evidenced by a large number of discovery calls and demos, coupled with a low close rate on those demos. A good coaching plan here would be a daily pipeline review of the salesperson's newly advanced opportunities, with a focus on the qualification of each opportunity.

2. *Time management:* Maybe this salesperson isn't managing his time well. Perhaps he's doing too much research on very early-stage opportunities. Perhaps his CRM skills are weak, or he's creating lots of unnecessary administrative work for himself. This diagnosis would be evidenced by below average volumes throughout the entire funnel (leads, demos, and customers). A possible coaching plan here would be to outline daily and weekly activity goals, have the salesperson block time in his calendar for each type of activity, and have him report back regularly on progress.

3. *Personal motivation:* Maybe this salesperson is just not bringing his "A" game to work every day. Maybe the average salesperson puts in a solid 50 hours per week, but this person is investing only 30. Again, this diagnosis would be illustrated by low volume through-out the entire funnel. A good coaching plan here is to have a personal conversation with the salesperson about why he comes to work every day. How much does he want to earn? What would he do with the money if he achieved his goal? By when does he want the money? Help him establish the connection between goal achievement and daily activity volume. Finally, set up a plan to review his progress daily.

4. *Call reluctance:* Maybe the salesperson has a fear of picking up the phone. That's a really tough one to fix, and probably indicates a failure in the recruiting funnel. It may require a fundamental shift in person-ality—or it may mean the "salesperson" is in the wrong profession.

Now let's look at the salesperson represented by the upper right diagonal pattern, listed as the top most person on the charts. She worked a good number of leads, but she had the lowest number of demos and, in turn, the lowest number of customers. Here are some possible diagnoses and coaching plans for this type of team member:

1. *Prospecting depth:* Maybe this salesperson isn't working her leads deeply enough. Perhaps she is only "touching" the leads once or twice before moving on. We can diagnose further by reviewing the CRM prospecting logs for the leads she has touched. From a coaching perspective, she probably needs some guidance on the

right prospecting cadence and how to leverage the CRM so nothing falls through the cracks.

2. *Lack of prospecting personalization:* Perhaps she's calling her leads deeply, but she's sending the same email and leaving the same voicemail each time. She needs to personalize each of those emails and voicemails to each prospect's context and build on her overall message each time. We can diagnose further by reviewing the content of her emails. If they are generic, then she must do more to add personalized context to each touch point. Salespeople need to leverage this context and deliver the most helpful information at the most helpful time.

3. *Trust development on the connect call:* Perhaps she's doing a great job contacting her leads and getting them on the phone. However, she's not engaging well with the prospects once she gets them on the phone. She may be leading with a boring elevator pitch every time, rather than using the calls to learn more about her prospects. Diagnosing this skill requires a tactical effort by the sales manager, which I will cover in a few pages when I discuss the process of "peeling back the onion." For coaching, set up two 90-minute shadowing sessions to listen in on her prospecting and connect calls. Role-play with her, using suggested improvements to her tactics, and then have her apply those improvements as you shadow her next few calls.

Finally, let's take a look at the salesperson represented by the upper left diagonal pattern, listed as the bottom most person on the charts. He's doing really well with high volumes of leads worked and demos delivered. However, he has a very low number of customers closed, especially for that amount of activity. Here are possible diagnoses and coaching plans for this salesperson:

1. *Lack of urgency:* This is the most common issue I encounter, whether it's at HubSpot or any of the many organizations I have helped. The prospect expresses great excitement about the product. They literally tell the salesperson they plan to buy. The next day, they call back and have some excuse about an upcoming trade show or

some deadline that's fast approaching. They ask you to call back in a month. When you call back a month later, they barely remember your name. A great way to surface this diagnosis is to review "closed lost" reasons on late-stage opportunities. Two solid coaching tactics include role-playing how to develop urgency on future opportunities and recording sales calls that can be reviewed and critiqued. The key questions here are: Why does this prospect need our product today? What will be the implications if they don't buy today? Imagine it is six months from now and the problem we're talking about solving is still not solved. What happens then? Will it really be that bad? If the answer is "no," then the salesperson has not developed the urgency and probably won't win that business.

2. *Lack of "decision maker" access:* In some cases the salesperson isn't identifying or reaching the decision maker. Often times, if a prospective buyer says he is the decision maker, he probably isn't. Conversely, true decision makers may try to deflect this ownership to someone else. Figuring out if a prospective buyer is really the decision maker is often tricky. A manager can diagnose a "lack of decision maker" issue by evaluating how long it has been since a salesperson directly engaged with the individual who has been identified as responsible for signing key documents. If that person turns out to be the CEO and we haven't yet spoken to her, we have an issue. Role-playing around specific opportunities works well to overcome this skill deficiency. I find that,on a case-by-case basis, the best salespeople appreciate the difference between why the end user wants our product and why the related decision maker wants our product. Best-in-class salespeople will alter the way they communicate value to each party so that everyone's interests feel addressed.

3. *Digging below the surface pain:* Perhaps the salesperson hasn't yet fully appreciated the prospect's pain. When I inquire about an opportunity's pain point and the salesperson says he needs more leads, we have an issue. Everybody needs more leads. Use probing questions to get to the deeper, underlying pain points. Why do they need more leads? How many leads do they generate today? How many do they need? How did they come up with that goal? Is this a "must-hit" goal or an "ideal world" goal?

"Peeling Back the Onion"

An important concept related to metrics-driven sales coaching is what I call "peeling back the onion." As we review each salesperson's high-level funnel metrics and begin to identify the areas of concern for each salesperson, the first question I ask myself is "How can we use deeper metrics to peel back the onion and properly diagnose the skill deficiency?"

The numbers rarely lie.

Figure 7.3 illustrates an example of "peeling back the onion." Remember the salesperson represented by the upper left diagonal pattern who worked lots of leads but struggled with conversion to the demo stage? Let's peel back the onion on this leads-worked-to-demos-booked ratio. Let's break down the data a bit, and look separately at the leads-worked-to-connects ratio and the connects-to-demos-booked ratio. This deeper view will help us to properly

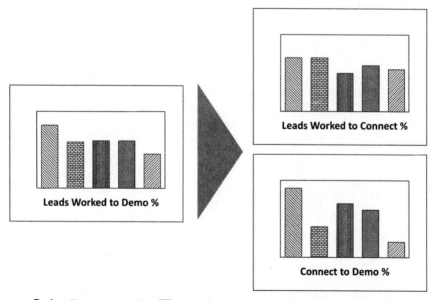

Each pattern represents a different salesperson's performance in a given month

Figure 7.3   Example of "Peeling Back the Onion" on a Skill Deficiency

diagnose her skill deficiency. If the leads-worked-to-connects ratio is low, then she is struggling to get people onto the phone. We need to dive into her prospecting frequency and personalization. If the connects-to-demos-booked ratio is low, then she is struggling to pique the prospect's interest on the connect calls. We need to listen to those calls in order to further diagnose.

"Peeling back the onion" saves us time in isolating individual skill deficiencies and gives us confidence that we're working on the right areas.

Measure the Coaching Success

How do we know if our coaching model is working? We measure it, of course! Figure 7.4 looks similar to the figures we discussed

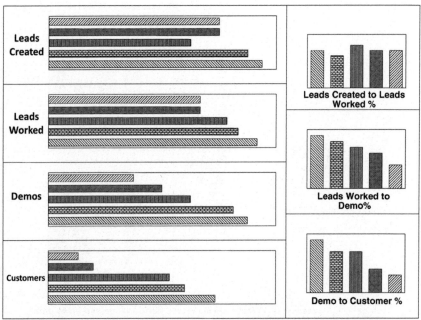

Each pattern represents sequential months in one salesperson's performance

Figure 7.4   Comparing Sales Funnel Activity of One Salesperson across a Number of Months

previously. However, rather than comparing the funnel across different ent salespeople within a set time frame, this chart shows how the funnel metrics change month over month for an individual salesperson. This enables us to go back to our coaching plans from prior months, review the metrics that each plan was intended to improve, and see if those metrics did in fact move. As you can see in Figure 7.4, which is based on the data of an actual HubSpot salesperson, this salesperson and her manager have been quite successful employing this process.

To Recap

- Effective sales coaching by sales managers is the most important lever to drive sales productivity.
- A common sales management mistake is to overwhelm the salesperson with coaching too many skills simultaneously. Pick one skill and focus.
- Use metrics to diagnose which skill development area will have the biggest impact on a salesperson's performance. Customize the coaching plan to that skill area. Execute metrics-driven sales coaching.

8

Motivation through Sales Compensation Plans and Contests

Whether you're a CEO or a VP of sales, the sales compensation plan is probably the most powerful tool in your tool chest. In thinking back to the critical strategic shifts HubSpot made as a business, most of them were executed via changes to the sales compensation plan.

People often ask me, "What is the best sales compensation structure to use?"

That is a very complicated question. The ideal plan is contextual not only to

> *"The sales compensation plan is one of the most effective tools for the CEO and VP of sales to drive business strategy."*

the type of business, but also to the stage of growth that business is in. In the first six years of HubSpot's growth, we utilized three different sales compensation plans, each of which was appropriate for the stage the business was in at the time.

I've provided a description of these plans ahead.

Plan 1: The Hunting Plan

The first compensation plan we ever had at HubSpot was very oriented toward "hunting" new customers. It was the right plan for the time. We had 100 customers. We were at an annual run rate of barely $300K. We needed to acquire customers quickly so that we could accelerate our path toward product/market fit and gain a deeper understanding of what could make our business model sustainable!

The first plan paid each salesperson $2 upfront for every $1 of monthly recurring revenue they brought on. For example, if a salesperson closed a customer on a $500 per month subscription, the salesperson earned a one-time $1,000 sales commission for that deal.

To protect the company from customer churn, we implemented a four-month claw-back on the commission. This meant that if the customer churned within the first four months, HubSpot took the entire commission back (deducted from the salesperson's next month of earned commissions). After his clients reached four months on the platform, the salesperson would keep the entire commission even if the customer canceled any time after four months.

This plan was simple, clean, and hunting-oriented.

The plan worked well to accelerate the velocity of new customer acquisition. HubSpot scaled from 100 to 1,000 customers in fewer than six months. We had grown the annual run rate to $3 million. Beautiful!

However, there are typically side effects for every commission plan. This certainly was the case with our hunting plan. As you might expect, customer churn exploded to an alarming, unsustainable level. Guess which month in a customer's life cycle had the highest churn. Month five, of course, right after the claw-back had expired. Was this a coincidence? I think not.

The sales compensation plan drives the results of the business.

Plan 2: The Customer Success Plan

The customer retention issue needed to be addressed. First we leaned into the data in order to understand the situation further. At the time, each new customer was being assigned a post-sale consultant, who would help them get set up and trained to be successful using our service. Our first theory was that some of the post-sale consultants were doing a better job than others. If we could identify which consultants were most successful, we could dig into the consultant's process, understand what they were doing differently, and introduce the superior processes across the team. However, when we analyzed the customer churn by post-sale consultant, the levels were similar across the team. This particular theory had not checked out.

Next, we analyzed customer churn rates by salesperson. Eureka! Here was our answer. Across the sales organization, there was more than a 10-fold difference between the salesperson with the lowest churn rate and the salesperson with the highest churn rate. We did not have a customer onboarding problem. We had a sales problem. Our customer retention was predicated on the types of customers the salespeople chose to target and the expectations they set with each new account.

I immediately shared the analysis with the sales team, illustrating each salesperson's churn rates and how they compared to the rest of the team. I educated them on the importance of retention to our business as well as to our customers. I informed them that I would be adjusting the sales compensation plan the following quarter, in order to align their customer churn performance with their commission checks.

Sure enough, next quarter, I followed through on my promise. I stack-ranked the sales team from the salesperson with the best churn rate right down to the salesperson with the worst churn rate. I then segmented the team into quartiles. The top performing quartile (top 25 percent) that used to earn $2 per $1 of monthly recurring revenue now earned $4 per $1 of monthly recurring revenue. "Congratulations," I said to them. "I am doubling your commission payments. Why? Because you bring on the best customers. Keep it up."

I moved on to the next quartile in the list. "Good work. You now earn $3 per $1 of monthly recurring revenue, a 50 percent increase above your previous rate."

"For the folks in the third quartile, there is no change. You will be paid the same rate of $2 per $1 of monthly recurring revenue."

I concluded with the final and most difficult message. "For the fourth and worst-performing quartile, your earnings are cut to $1 per $1 of monthly recurring revenue. Why? Your customers are not succeeding. On average, they are unprofitable for our company. More importantly, you are wasting our customers' money by not setting proper expectations on how they can succeed with our service. We have initiated training over the last month on better customer expectation setting. We need you to take that training seriously. We are here to help you through this skill development."

Within six months, churn had dropped by 70 percent.

The sales compensation plan drives the results of the business.

Plan 3: The Customer Commitment Plan

About 18 months later, Plan 2 (the Customer Success Plan) had run its course. In the past, "poor expectation setting from sales" had dominated the list of reasons why customers churned. As Plan 2 took effect, "poor expectation setting from sales" was almost nonexistent on the churn reason list. Churn in general was far lower and the cancellation reasons were not alarming—customers were acquired by larger companies, isolated product bugs, and so forth. Overall, this was a great outcome for the business. However, because the sales compensation plan was still highly correlated to customer churn and because most of the remaining customer churns that were occurring occurred for reasons outside of the salesperson's control, the plan was no longer effective at rewarding salesperson behavior. At this point, all of the salespeople were proficient at setting good expectations with their customers. The salespeople who ranked best on the customer churn list were no longer the best expectation setters. Instead, they had good luck. A change in the sales compensation plan was necessary.

I needed to keep customer churn in check. I also needed the salespeople to be able to control their own destiny. I asked myself, "What criterion is 100 percent in the control of the salesperson and highly correlated with customer success?"

For the HubSpot business at the time, the answer was advanced payment terms for new customers. Our customers who paid month-to-month were less committed to the overall HubSpot service and were far more likely to churn. Those who prepaid annually were more committed to the service and were ultimately more successful.

As a result, Plan 3 was designed as follows:

1. Salespeople would earn $2 per $1 of monthly recurring revenue
2. The commission would be paid out as follows:
   a. 50 percent on the first month's payment
   b. 25 percent on the sixth month's payment
   c. 25 percent on the twelfth month's payment

Under this plan, if a customer signed up paying month-to-month, the salesperson would need to wait an entire year to earn the full commission from that customer. If the customer signed up paying a year in advance, the salesperson would earn the entire commission immediately. The plan was well aligned with how far in advance the customer paid. How far in advance a customer paid was correlated with high customer success and completely in control of the salesperson.

Before rolling out this plan, the average prepayment commitment was 2.5 months. When I rolled out this plan, that average jumped

"There is no perfect sales compensation plan. The appropriate sales compensation plan depends on the stage of the business."

to seven months. Customer churn remained in check; in fact it improved. Customers were profitable to HubSpot. Salespeople felt like they were in control of their destiny. Mission accomplished.

Am I recommending the same evolution of compensation plans for your business? Absolutely not. As I mentioned, the sales compensation plan depends highly on the type of business you're in, and the stage of business you're at. I hope the foregoing history illustrates this point and provides real-world examples of plans and their respective impact.

Criteria to Evaluate a New Commission Plan

Evaluate a sales compensation design through the lens of three factors: Simple. Aligned. Immediate.

Let me elaborate.

- *Simple:* Salespeople should not need a spreadsheet to calculate their plan. If too many variables are included, salespeople may become confused about which behaviors will drive the largest commission check. They might throw the plan aside and just go sell the way they know best. The opportunity to drive the desired behavior through the compensation plan is lost. Keep the plan simple. It should be extraordinarily clear which outcomes you are rewarding.
- *Aligned:* Look ahead to the next year and ask yourself, "What is the most important goal the company needs to achieve? Customer count? Profitability? Customer success? Market share? New product distribution? New market penetration?" Then ask yourself, "How can the sales compensation plan be aligned with this goal?" Do not underestimate the power of the compensation

plan. You can tweak sales training, redesign marketing materials, attend customer conferences—you name it. Regardless of these efforts, if the majority of your company's revenue is generated from a sales team, properly aligning the sales compensation plan will be the most impactful tool in your company's tool chest.

- *Immediate:* When salespeople succeed, they should see that success reflected in their paycheck immediately. When they fail, they should feel the pain in their paycheck immediately. Any delay between good (or bad) behavior and the related financial outcome will decrease the impact of the plan.

> *"Evaluate a sales compensation design through the lens of three factors: Simple. Aligned. Immediate."*

Involve the Sales Team in Compensation Plan Design

One factor in the success of our evolving compensation plan was my decision to involve the sales team in the design process. I usually held what we called a "town meeting" to initiate involvement of the sales team. The town meeting was a forum for me to share why we were changing the plan and communicate the goals of the newest structure. The meeting was optional, although I can assure you it was well attended. After communicating the plan goals, I opened up the floor to structural ideas from the team. The brainstorming began. As the meeting progressed, I shared some of the structures that were being considered. I opened the floor to their feedback.

As a follow-up to the town meeting, I often initiated a page on the company wiki, reiterating the reasons for changing the plan, stating the goals of the new plan, and showing some of the structures that were being considered. The conversation continued online with ideas and reactions. I responded to most comments. This digital format allowed salespeople to catch up on and participate in the conversation when they had time.

Of course, throughout both the town meeting and the wiki posting, I was very explicit that the commission plan design was not a democratic process. For example, the plan would not be put to a vote. It was critical for the sales team to not confuse transparency and involvement with an invitation to selfishly design the plan around their individual needs. I had to protect the interests of HubSpot as an organization, not just help salespeople maximize their commission checks.

All in all, this process of involving the sales team was quite effective. By informing the team up front of the reasons for and goals of the new plan, I prepared them psychologically for the change that was coming. Most of them greatly appreciated the transparency, even when changes were not favorable to their individual situations. During the process, the sales team contributed some great ideas. Every commission plan change we made included at least one structural element that had originated from one of our salespeople during these discussions. Each idea that was incorporated was legitimately help-ful—we weren't simply trying to appease the team by accepting their input regardless of quality. The discussions also helped me further understand the perspectives of the salespeople, isolate the main concerns they had with the discussion format, and familiarize myself with the components about which they felt most strongly. When the new commission plan was finally rolled out, our involved approach enabled the sales team to have a deep understanding of why the final structure was chosen. They understood why some of their ideas hadn't been included, since even the rejected ideas had been discussed in the "town meeting" or on the wiki thread.

Promotion Tiers: Removing the Subjectivity from Promotions and Compensation Adjustments

Besides the commission plan, there was another important element of the sales compensation structure: a formalized career growth plan. Some salespeople want to develop their leadership skills. Some want to grow their ownership over entrepreneurial aspects of their job. Some salespeople have no desire to become managers or change products; they just want to grow as individual contributors and hone their craft. A common career goal for salespeople involves the movement from inside sales to outside sales. However, in the first few years of HubSpot, we did not have any outside opportunities. We were purposely focused on the large, untapped SMB market, and felt the best way to reach our future customers was by focusing exclusively on building an inside sales team. I needed an alternative solution to provide a career track for our salespeople.

Most organizations relied on an annual review and traditional 2 to 4 percent increase in salary based on performance. That approach felt too subjective to me. The performance of a salesperson is so measurable; I felt I could come up with something more quantifiable and more motivating.

I came up with the concept of promotional tiers. Figure 8.1 shows an example set of these tiers. I have altered these metrics from actual HubSpot data, but the figure illustrates the point.

Title	Compensation	Requirements for Promotion to Next Level
Principal Sales Associate	$40K Base $60K Variable 15K additional options	> $210K MRR Install Base > $7K MRR per Month > 8 Months Upfront Payment
Senior Sales Associate	$40K Base $50K Variable 10K additional options	> $130K MRR Install Base > $6K MRR per Month > 7 Months Upfront Payment
Sales Associate	$40K Base $40K Variable 5K options	> $60K MRR Install Base > $5K MRR per Month > 6 Months Upfront Payment

Figure 8.1   Example of Salesperson Promotion Tiers

The first column in the chart illustrates the salesperson's title at each level. The second column illustrates the base pay, variable pay, and additional equity earned at each level. The third column illustrates the criteria necessary to make it to the next level. According to Figure 8.1, the entry-level sales title is "sales associate." To get promoted to the senior sales associate, an entry-level salesperson needs to accumulate an install base of $60K in monthly recurring revenue (MRR), acquire an average of $5K new MRR per month, and sign up new customers with an average of six months paid up front. Once the salesperson's performance meets these three criteria, she is promoted to senior sales associate. Her quota increases, but earnings per dollar closed increases as well, resulting in a higher commission rate and higher OTE. In addition, promoted salespeople receive an additional 10,000 stock options.

The promotion tiers were a powerful structure within the overall sales compensation model. Salespeople are competitive, financially motivated, and always looking to achieve goals. They took these tiers seriously, always looking to advance to the next level. As a result, the promotion criteria represented another opportunity for me to align compensation with the desired behaviors I wanted from our salespeople.

The promotion tiers were also great for culture. We did not have to manage annual reviews and the often-arbitrary compensation increases. The promotion tiers took the subjectivity and politics out of this process and empowered the salespeople to ascend as quickly as they could. Feedback was delivered on a weekly and monthly basis, and was not reliant on the annual review.

One important observation here was the fact that tenure was not a criterion for promotion. This strategy was very important to me. Many top performers achieved the promotion in as few as seven months. For others, it took over two years. I had no problem with that. Frankly, I never understood why tenure was a factor for promotion in so many sales organizations. Sales is such a measurable, meritocratic function that I simply left tenure out.

Using Sales Contests to Motivate the Team

"Mark, I need to get our sales activity up. My salespeople just won't make enough dials. What should I do?"

Run a contest.

"Mark, my team is terrible at forecasting. They do not take it seriously. They do not follow our best practices. What should I do?"

Run a contest.

"Mark, we just launched a mission-critical product into the market this quarter. However, our sales team is stuck in their old ways of selling. What should I do?"

Run a contest.

If the sales compensation plan is Batman, the sales contest is Robin. Contests are *almost* as effective as the compensation plan when it comes to motivating the sales team and driving the desired behavior. Contests bring a fun, dynamic aspect to a sometimes mundane daily routine. Contests can be aligned with desired behaviors and, unlike commission plans, can be temporary and short-term focused. Contests can even be used to build team culture.

> *"Sales contests are an effective tool to drive short-term behaviors and build team culture within the sales organization."*

For these reasons, I ran a sales contest almost every month, especially in the early years of team development. Here are the six best practices I found most effective for sales contest design.

1. *Align the contest with a short-term behavior change desired for the majority of the team.* Like sales commission plans, sales contests are a great way to drive home desired behavior. For example, you may fear a summer slump and want to boost activity in June. This desire would be difficult to pull off through the commission plan. However, an activity-based contest in June would do the trick.

2. *Make the contest team-based.* If there are 12 people on the sales team, form four teams of three salespeople and have the teams compete rather than have every man for himself. This approach has a remarkable impact on team culture, especially in the early phases of team building. For the first three years at HubSpot, every contest I ran was a team contest. The positive impact on team culture was remarkable. I would often see high-performing salespeople help out their teammates who were lagging behind. The salespeople who were lagging behind worked late in order to avoid letting their teams down. After three years of team-based contests, I finally ran a contest based on individual performance. For the first time, I witnessed accusations of cheating and saw backstabbing behavior on the floor. We immediately returned to team contests.

3. *Make the prize team-based.* In addition to making the contest team-based, choose a reward that the team experiences together. Rent a limo to take them to the casino, buy them a golf outing, or send them sailing for a day. Making the prize team-based maximizes the positive impact on culture. Not only does the team win together, they experience the reward together. They return to the office with photos of the great time they had . . . together. People feel good about their colleagues. Teams feel motivated to win the following month.

4. *Send out updated contest standings every night.* At least once per day, the contest standings should be published to the entire sales team, if not to the entire company! This is such a critical execution point. Without daily updates, contest effectiveness will drop precipitously. Even if it means compiling and posting the results manually, publish the results every day.

5. *Choose the time frame wisely.* The time frame needs to be long enough to drive home the desired behavior change but short enough that salespeople stay engaged. A daily time frame is too short. Weekly contests are on the briefer end of acceptable. A quarterly time frame is probably too long. Monthly contests are ideal.

6. *Avoid contest fever.* Don't read this section and implement five simultaneous contests. Overlapping contests will dilute each other. Run one contest at a time for a given group of salespeople.

The Best Contest I Ever Ran

As the HubSpot sales team scaled and our business hit a new stage of maturity, sales forecasting became more important. Unfortunately, as is the case with many sales organizations, the HubSpot sales team was not good at forecasting, and they didn't take the task seriously.

So, I devised the following contest:

1. I separated everyone into four contest teams.
2. Every time a salesperson conducted a product demo for a prospect, he had to estimate, by the end of the day, whether that prospect would close by the end of the month.
3. If the salesperson thought the prospect would become a customer that month, he would write the prospect's name on a whiteboard, accompanied by a "confidence score" between 0 and 100. This figure represented the level of confidence the salesperson had in his guess.
4. At the end of the month, we reviewed the whiteboard. For each prospect who actually became a customer, the confidence score was added to the salesperson's score and, in turn, their team's score. Just as importantly, for any prospects that did not become customers but had been added to the board, the associated confidence score was subtracted from the individual and team scores.

Guess what the winning team's score was? *Negative 70!*

The proof is in the pudding.

The team had not appreciated how bad they were at forecasting until this contest illustrated the situation. They had had "happy ears" after their discovery calls and demos, thinking every prospect was sure to buy. They had been skipping steps in their discovery and qualification processes, leading to sloppy pipeline management. As we reran the contest and provided forecasting training, behavior improved and team scores increased.

To Recap

- The sales compensation plan is one of the most effective tools for the CEO and VP of sales to use to drive business strategy.
- There is no perfect sales compensation plan. The appropriate sales compensation plan depends on the stage of the business.
- Evaluate a sales compensation design through the lens of three factors: Simple. Aligned. Immediate.
- Sales contests are an effective tool to drive short-term behaviors and build team culture within the sales organization.

---

9 | Developing Sales Leaders— Advantages of a "Promote from Within" Culture

"Don't promote your best salespeople to sales management."

Ask a seasoned sales executive about developing sales managers and this statement will probably be the first words out of her mouth.

The statement certainly has merit. Of all the professional functions within an organization (e.g., marketing, product, finance, HR, and so forth), sales has the largest variance between the general characteristics that are conducive to success on the front line and the general characteristics that are conducive to success in the management ranks. Sometimes really good salespeople are selfish, egotistical, and competitive by nature. Those traits do not translate well into management.

However, will promoting the worst salespeople to sales management work?

Of course not. How could a salesperson respect the coaching from a manager who couldn't do the job himself?

What about the strategy of hiring experienced managers from the outside?

That might work for other companies, but I didn't see it working for me at HubSpot, given our unique buyer context. Sure, if I had been able to find sales managers who had successfully led teams that sold a similar value proposition to a similar buyer profile with a similar sales playbook, I might have hired them. However, that did not work out for me. Not only did I fail to find any sales managers with experience leading teams selling the value proposition of HubSpot, but also I failed to find any who ran the sales management model I wanted. Most of the sales managers I met ran what I would refer to as a "sweatshop." They drilled their salespeople with daily required activity metrics. They told salespeople to "just get me on the phone with a qualified prospect" and closed the business for them. They spent most of their day inspecting forecasts and pipelines. They were not great coaches. They were not very analytical. They did not relate particularly well to their people.

So what is the best way to build a layer of sales managers?

This was precisely the question I faced not even six months into the job at HubSpot. The sales team had already expanded to eight salespeople. We continued to add a new salesperson each month. I needed a solution quickly.

Ultimately, I decided to develop the sales management layer from within by training and promoting the folks I already had on my team. These people knew our buyer persona. They knew our product's value proposition. They knew the sales system in which we were operating. It was my best bet.

In order to develop my frontline salespeople into managers, I set out to establish a sales management course. I read a number of sales management books but few resonated with me. I took a moment to reflect on the key management skills I wanted these managers to possess as they embarked on the role at HubSpot. Coaching. Negative feedback delivery. Team motivation. Conflict management. These were the skills the managers needed.

I realized I wasn't just looking for management skills; I was looking for leadership skills. I redirected my research efforts and suddenly the material I was finding started to click. It was not long before I had assembled a 12-week sales leadership course.

The 12-week sales leadership course curriculum is listed here. I recommend focusing more on the categories of skills rather than the HubSpot-specific resource guides themselves, though I have included them for context.

> *"Focus on leadership skills, rather than general sales management skills, when developing future managers internally."*

1. Defining and Developing Your Leadership Style
   - "Discovering Your Authentic Leadership" (http://www.aawccnatl.org/assets/authentic%20leadership.pdf)
   - *Building an Authentic Leadership Image* (http://solutions.ccl.org/Building_an_Authentic_Leadership_Image)
   - *Twelve O'Clock High* (www.amazon.com/Twelve-OClock-High-Gregory-Peck/dp/B00005PJ8V)
   - *Forceful Leadership and Enabling Leadership: You Can Do Both* (http://solutions.ccl.org/Forceful_Leadership_and_Enabling_Leadership_You_Can_Do_Both)
   - *Ongoing Feedback: How to Get It, How to Use It* (http://solutions.ccl.org/Ongoing_Feedback_How_to_Get_It_How_to_Use_It)
2. Providing Positive and Negative Feedback to Subordinates
   - *Feedback That Works: How to Build and Deliver Your Message* (http://solutions.ccl.org/Feedback_That_Works_How_to_Build_and_Deliver_Your_Message)
   - *Giving Feedback to Subordinates* (http://solutions.ccl.org/Giving_Feedback_to_Subordinates)
3. Successful Mentoring and Coaching
   - *Sales Coaching: Making the Great Leap from Sales Manager to Sales Coach* (www.amazon.com/Sales-Coaching-Making-Great-Manager/dp/0071603808)
   - *Seven Keys to Successful Mentoring* (http://solutions.ccl.org/Seven_Keys_to_Successful_Mentoring)

- *One Minute Manager* (www.amazon.com/Minute-Manager-Ph-D-Kenneth-Blanchard/dp/0425098478)
- *Succeed—How We Can Reach Our Goals* (www.amazon.com/Succeed-How-Can-Reach-Goals/dp/0452297710)

4. Managing Conflict
   - *Managing Conflict with Direct Reports* (http://solutions.ccl.org/Managing_Conflict_with_Direct_Reports)
   - *Managing Conflict with Peers* (http://solutions.ccl.org/Managing_Conflict_with_Peers)
   - *Managing Conflict with Your Boss* (http://solutions.ccl.org/Managing_Conflict_with_Your_Boss)

5. Managing through Change
   - *Adaptability: Responding Effectively to Change* (http://solutions.ccl.org/Adaptability_Responding_Effectively_to_Change)

6. Building and Developing Your Team
   - *Good to Great*: Chapter 3, First Who . . . Then What (www.amazon.com/gp/product/0066620996#noop)
   - *Raising Sensitive Issues in a Team* (http://solutions.ccl.org/Raising_Sensitive_Issues_in_a_Team)
   - *Building Your Team's Morale, Pride, and Spirit* (http://solutions.ccl.org/Building_Your_Teams_Morale_Pride_and_Spirit)

7. Active Listening
   - *Active Listening: Improve Your Ability to Listen and Lead* (http://solutions.ccl.org/Active_Listening_Improve_Your_Ability_to_Listen_and_Lead)

> *"Develop your leadership bench by using a formal leadership curriculum for your salespeople who earn the opportunity."*

Participants were asked to complete the following three tasks:

1. Each week, leadership candidates started by completing a preparation document related to the topic of the week. For example, if the week's topic was "conflict management," then the preparation document would pose some representative conflict scenarios and prompt the leadership candidates to explain how they would deal

with each scenario. The preparation work was effective for testing the natural instincts of the leadership candidates and getting them to think about these scenarios before exposing them to best practices around handling them.

2. After the preparation work was submitted, leadership candidates completed the reading(s) assigned for that week's topic. Candidates could connect the general best practices to actual scenarios they would surely face as sales managers.

3. After completing the reading, candidates met with me (or, once we had reached scale, a full-time leadership trainer) to role-play the scenarios in person. The role-play was an opportunity to evaluate how well the candidates absorbed and applied the best practices.

Here are some example role-plays that correspond with the topics covered in leadership training.

■ *Providing Negative Feedback Effectively:* "You just shadowed a demo with one of your salespeople. The call was awful. The salesperson vomited product features the entire time and demonstrated inferior product knowledge. No qualifying questions were asked. We will role-play this situation in the next session."

■ *Managing Conflict with Direct Reports:* "One of your salespeople signed up two new customers and both customers cancelled almost immediately. In both cases, the salesperson's commission was clawed back. It is clear that expectation setting issues occurred during both sales processes. However, the salesperson is aggressively claiming that both cancellations are the fault of the post-sale account manager for mismanaging the on-boarding process. We will role-play this situation in the next session."

■ *Building Team Spirit and Pride:* "For the second quarter in a row, the team has missed goal. Fewer than 50 percent of your salespeople are actually making their quota. You have heard that some members of the team have started interviewing outside of the company. You need to lift your team's spirits. We will role-play this situation in the next session."

■ *Active Listening:* "One of your salespeople grabs you in the hallway and requests to change teams. Given the seriousness of the request, you inform the salesperson that you are running into a meeting right now but you would like to meet with him immediately afterwards. We will role-play this discussion in our next session."

Prerequisites for Leadership Consideration

Simply accumulating tenure on the HubSpot sales team did not automatically grant a salesperson entry into the sales leadership curriculum. Entry had to be earned. There were three skill areas we evaluated as a prerequisite to the leadership class: performance, sales skills, and leadership potential.

"Performance" was the easiest to evaluate— for example, "Exceed the sales targets for six months in a row and you have fulfilled the 'performance' prerequisite." It was not necessary to be the top performer, but consistent goal attainment was a must.

For "sales skills," I looked for well-roundedness. As discussed in Chapter 5, I had plenty of top salespeople who had "superpowers" but ranged anywhere from average to very good on other aspects of the sales process. For example, remember Bob from Chapter 5? He was pretty good at consultative selling, above average with his discovery calls, and had mediocre presentation skills. What was his superpower? Bob was an activity hound. His volume really set him apart from the pack and made him our top monthly salesperson on several occasions. If I promoted Bob to manager, how would he ever effectively develop a salesperson who was struggling with their discovery call? The only way Bob would succeed as a manager is if he found eight salespeople whose strengths perfectly matched his own. That would be nearly impossible, and certainly would not scale.

I needed sales leadership candidates who had a well-rounded grasp of the entire sales methodology. Sales leaders with balanced abilities would be able to diagnose a specific issue and be qualified to customize a coaching plan to address the issue.

In order to assess a leadership candidate's "sales skill" well-roundedness, I leveraged the sales skill certifications developed for new hire training. I simply created a more advanced level for each skill area. A sales leadership candidate met the "sales skill" prerequisite if they scored at or above all of the advanced levels.

Finally, "leadership potential" was demonstrated through a candidate's contribution to the team. It is not necessary to be a sales manager to demonstrate leadership among the team. Frontline salespeople might demonstrate leadership simply by contributing insightful questions and comments during team meetings. They could proactively mentor a new salesperson on the floor. They could own a particular class in new hire training or help administer new skill training for the current team. There were many ways that I could assess a candidate's "leadership potential" while he was still an individual contributor.

From the Classroom to the Real World

There was one final step before candidates could be promoted; they needed real-life experience hiring, developing, and managing a salesperson. Leadership candidates who made it through the sales leadership course were given the opportunity to hire their own salesperson. They interviewed prospective sales candidates and reported their thoughts back to management. They informed us which hire they would make. Once the new sales hire was made, leadership candidates were responsible for mentoring the new hire during training and managing them for their first two months on the floor. Of course, as a support layer, we were there to advise the leadership candidates accordingly.

This approach gave sales leadership candidates a real-life taste of the day-to-day management role. They could better evaluate if they were heading down the right track before making the final leap. This exercise also provided a relatively safe

"Before formal promotion, let qualified leadership candidates hire, train, and manage one new salesperson while still carrying their individual quota responsibilities."

environment for any final skill development. If a leadership candidate made a mistake, he would lose credibility with only one salesperson. Better to experience a "miss" with a single mentee than fumble early on as a sales manager with an eight-person team.

One approach to developing leaders that I see in many organizations is the "team lead" position, in which a salesperson is simultaneously in charge of managing a small team and carrying an individual quota for an extended period of time. I am not a fan of this approach. In my observations, the "team lead" struggles to balance both aspects of their role. Either the management quality suffers or the individual's perform-ance suffers. Usually it is the management component. Therefore, in contrast to the traditional team lead structure, our structure, limited in duration and scope of responsibility, made me far more comfortable.

In fact, the temporary double-duty role effectively fosters the time management expertise essential to navigating the sales management role. When a leadership candidate is eventually promoted and has an eight-person team, how much time will he actually be able to commit to each salesperson? Realistically, three to four hours per week. By temporarily juggling a quota and the oversight of an individual, the leadership candidate has an opportunity to practice the art of time management as a coach.

Common Potholes from New Sales Managers

Effective Time Management

Susan was promoted to sales manager two months ago. Back in the day, she was a star as a salesperson—a great funnel manager, always organized, always well-rested. Her attitude offered a glowing "pick-me-up" for everyone around her in the office.

Not anymore—not since her promotion to sales manager. I peered over at the new Susan and saw a harried-looking, red-eyed, burned-out professional. I wish I could say I was surprised. I almost always saw this situation unfold for newly promoted sales managers.

New managers have an unrealistic perception of how much coaching they can actually do with each of their team members. They need to learn quickly that success as a manager is about the efficiency of their coaching—their ability to diagnose the issues, customize a coaching plan, and execute the coaching in a time efficient manner.

"Susan, what is wrong?" I asked.

Almost out of breath, Susan responded, "Oh, Mark. There just aren't enough hours in the day. I feel like I am being pulled in a million directions and before I know it, it is 7 p.m. and the day is over. How do managers do it?"

I have an exercise I take new sales managers through at this stage of their transition. Here was the perfect opportunity.

"Susan, do me a favor," I responded. "Write on the whiteboard all of the professional tasks you do each week. Think of the different categories of work. You coach your reps. You attend management meetings and hold team meetings. You are involved with some deals. You check email. Write them all down. Now write the approximate hours per week you spend on each task. What is the total number of hours per week?"

"102!" Susan exclaimed.

"No wonder you are going crazy," I pointed out. "You need to cut back, but where? There are a few team meetings each week that need to happen. Obviously, email cannot pile up so that time is necessary. It seems like you have the right amount of time allocated to overseeing your team's opportunities. In reality, the only thing that we can touch is the time you spend coaching each salesperson. You listed six hours per week per person, but with an eight-person team, you simply can't

> *"New sales managers need to appreciate how in-demand their coaching time is, and must be efficient with their coaching execution."*

spare that much time. You need to find a way to be more efficient with your coaching."

The Manager as a Glorified Salesperson

Almost all sales managers were individual contributors at some point in their careers. On the front line, they controlled their own destiny. If they got into trouble one quarter, it was not a problem. They would simply increase their own activity and get back on track.

As these salespeople transition to management, they lose that direct control. They must achieve their goals through the salespeople on their teams. This new paradigm can be a frustrating and difficult transition for folks who used to control their own destinies.

So what do they do? They start doing the important calls for their salespeople. "Just set me up with your next demo. I'll run it for you. I'll get the deal done."

This dynamic is dangerous, as the manager ends up smothering and spoiling her salespeople. Because they are no longer closing deals themselves, the salespeople start to lose confidence in their own abilities. They also grow apathetic. "Hey, if I can just bring my manager on every call, she'll get me to quota or fail. Either way, it's not my fault."

This approach simply does not scale. Managers need to be patient with their salespeople. As a manager, it is painful to hear a salesperson mishandle an objection and not speak up, but it's essential to that salesperson's development. He needs to skin his knees. The coaching will come afterwards. Managers need to teach salespeople how to get themselves out of trouble and stay productive without too

> "Avoid the common pitfalls of new managers: exhibiting weak time management around coaching, acting as a glorified salesperson, and giving up on new hires too early."

much hand-holding. They need to be efficient coaches. They need to diagnose skill deficiencies, devise custom coaching strategies, and coach effectively.

Giving Up on a Salesperson Too Early

It is such an amazing feeling when one of your new hires comes out of training crushing the phones, exceeding quota after quota, and maintaining a great attitude. All it took was a few simple nudges by you as her manager.

Unfortunately, not all hires work out that way. More often than not, I would receive reports from managers stating that their new sales hire "just wasn't working out." The more inexperienced the sales manager, the sooner I would receive the news.

Here's what worried me: When we remained patient and gave those "weak" salespeople another six months, many of the folks who supposedly "weren't working out" became rock stars in our sales organization. As a guy who loves predictability, my head was spinning.

Time and time again, I see managers giving up on new hires too early. Yes, we would all love it if new hires crushed it right out of training and never looked back. But often, the "weak" salespeople just need some effective coaching and someone to believe in them for a few months before everything starts to click.

In these cases, my advice to a sales manager is to pick a deficiency in a salesperson's process, coach them on it, and check in with them the next day. If the manager sees improvement and the improvement appears to stick, that is a promising sign. It may take some work, but the salesperson is demonstrating coachability and should be able to evolve into a productive individual contributor. However, if a manager coaches a salesperson on a simple deficiency and doesn't see the salesperson apply the coaching, that is a bad sign. It is probably best for both parties to part ways and let the individual contributor find a buyer context better suited for his strengths.

To Recap

- Focus on leadership skills, rather than general sales management skills, when developing future managers internally.
- Develop your leadership bench by using a formal leadership curriculum for your salespeople who earn the opportunity.
- Before formal promotion, let qualified leadership candidates hire, train, and manage one new salesperson while still carrying their individual quota responsibilities.
- Avoid the common pitfalls of new managers: exhibiting weak time management around coaching, acting as a glorified salesperson, and giving up on new hires too early.

PART IV

The Demand Generation Formula

10

Flip the Demand Generation Formula—Get Buyers to Find *You*

Have you been cold-called in the past six months? Did you enjoy the experience? Did you engage with the salesperson? Did you buy the product?

Have you recently received an unsolicited piece of direct mail or email? Did you open it? Did you like receiving it? Did you buy the product that was promoted?

Have you conducted a Google search to research a product in the past six months? Did you enjoy the process? Did you make a purchase?

Have you heard about a product in social media from people you trust? Did you look into the product? Did you end up buying it?

I have posed those questions to hundreds of audiences over the years. Some were MBA students. Some were doctors and lawyers. Some were tech entrepreneurs. Some were realtors. Regardless of the audience, the results of the survey are always the same. Very few hands go up when folks are asked whether a cold call or unsolicited email instigated a purchase. Almost all of the hands go up when people are asked whether a Google search or social media discussion influenced a purchase.

Buyers get annoyed with the interruptive tactics referred to in the first two sets of questions. At HubSpot, we call these tactics "outbound marketing." Outbound marketing just doesn't work anymore. Buyers dislike outbound marketing so much that they actually invest in technology to keep these tactics out of their lives. Buyers add themselves to the Do Not Call Registry. Buyers use DVRs to fast-forward through television commercials. Buyers keep unsolicited email out of their inboxes with spam blockers.

Today's buyers are empowered by the Internet. They are empowered by Google and social media. At HubSpot, we refer to these channels as "inbound marketing." Buyers do not need to talk to a salesperson, read an advertisement, or visit a booth at a trade show.

> *"Today's buyer is empowered by the Internet. A modern demand generation strategy means less focus on interruptive outbound marketing and more focus on inbound marketing."*

Buyers can be bored at home on a Saturday night and start researching the problems they are experiencing at work. This action is the start of the modern sales and marketing funnel.

Ironically, when I pose these same survey questions to sales and marketing executives, asking them where their companies are spending their sales and marketing dollars, the results are quite different.

"How much are you spending on outbound marketing, such as cold-calling, direct mail, advertising, and trade shows?"

Many people are embarrassed about the amount of money they are throwing away on these tactics.

"How much are you spending on inbound marketing, such as SEO, social media participation, and blogging?"

Many people are spending next to nothing.

Despite the shift from outbound marketing to inbound marketing that is so obvious when viewing the situation as a buyer, for whatever reason, companies are very slow to react. Companies watch the effectiveness of outbound marketing tactics decline. Companies watch the effectiveness of inbound marketing tactics increase. Yet companies continue to pour the majority of their demand generation efforts into outbound marketing.

Don't make this mistake. Invest in inbound marketing. Help buyers find you.

How Can Your Business Rank at the Top of Google?

There are hundreds of phrases for which every business owner would give their left arm in order to rank at the top of Google. The potential impact to their business is enormous.

How do you do it? How do you get your business to the top of Google for the words and phrases that your best-fit buyers are searching for?

Let's review a brief history of search engine ranking algorithms. You may recall that Google was not the first search engine. Do you remember Alta Vista and Excite? They were among the first movers in the search engine industry. These early search engines would read certain elements of a web page called metadata. These elements, such as meta-keywords, meta-descriptions, and page titles, are not always visible to a user. The first wave of search engines would simply search for these elements on a web page (i.e., "crawl the web page") and rank the search results based on the meta-content of the websites.

At first glance, this sounds like a logical approach. However, web marketers started to figure out how to cheat the system. They would put high traffic words like "baseball" in their meta-keywords just to attract traffic to their website. Over time, these tactics became known as "black hat" tactics. As these tactics became more popular and people became pros at "tricking" the search engine into ranking their website for a given term, the relevance of the search results to the original search terms declined substantially. The core value of search engines was being compromised.

Then Google came along. When devising its search engine, Google asked, "What attribute of a website can we use to automatically determine the website's relevance and authority?" Its conclusion was "inbound links." An inbound link is a hyperlink on another website that directs back to your website. I am sure you have seen many hyperlinks. They look like this: www.yourwebsite.com. Google figured that if a website had a lot of other people linking to it, the website being linked to must be pretty important. It is really hard to wake up one day, start a website, and immediately convince thousands of people to link back to it. To make the algorithm even more effective, Google was also able to factor in the importance of the website that was linking back to your website. For example, a link from the *Wall Street Journal* would be thousands of times more impactful than a link from your 16-year-old nephew's personal blog.

In addition to the quality and quantity of inbound links, the rise of social media has caused Google to factor social media influence into the algorithm. If your blog articles are often retweeted in social media, if your company's Twitter account has lots of followers, if your company's Facebook page has lots of fans, Google will pay attention. Just like inbound links, it is hard to fake a large following and lots of engagement with your content. If lots of people follow you and lots of people share your content across social media channels, Google figures there is a good chance you are a thought leader on a given topic and ranks you prominently in the search engine results for that topic.

In a nutshell, that is how search engines work. You need lots of inbound links. You need lots of social media authority. You cannot fake your way through it. You need to build your websites authentically. If you accomplish these goals, you will be found often by qualified prospects in Google. The demand for your business will grow exponentially. Your business will be changed forever.

At this point, you may be asking, "But how do I achieve these goals? How do I organically get a lot of inbound links from other websites? How do I organically build a large social media following?"

Here are the two simple actions you need to take in order to drive inbound links and social media following:

1. Create quality content (e.g., blogs, ebooks, webinars) on a frequent basis.
2. Participate in the social media discussions in which your target prospects are already conversing.

> *"Successful inbound marketing comes from two tactics: (1) continual quality content production, and (2) frequent online participation in social media where your target buyers are already conversing."*

That's it. This simple strategy will modernize your demand generation strategy. It will align your business with the habits of the modern buyer. It will get your business found by the prospects you care about most. Not only will you start generating lots of traffic from Google, you will also start developing a valuable social media following. You will start to amass a sizable blog subscriber list. Prospects will start to give you their email so you can continue to send them the valuable content you now regularly produce. These actions of blogging, quality content production, and social media participation to drive qualified Google search traffic is the foundation of inbound marketing. It is the cornerstone of getting your business found when and where your prospects are searching.

This Does Not Happen Overnight

One major mistake companies make when embarking on this journey is a lack of commitment. They set up a blog and social media accounts for the company. They write three blog articles. They promote their articles on their social media accounts. Nothing happens. They think, "Maybe inbound marketing doesn't work for my business?"

It will. You just need more time. We often draw an analogy between this style of demand generation and weight loss. If you have a goal to lose 10 pounds, you do not hit the gym three times in the first week and lose the 10 pounds. In fact, you probably remain the same weight. However, if you keep it up three times a week for a few months, you start to lose weight. You begin to feel better. Working out becomes part of your routine. You can no longer imagine a week without getting to the gym a few times. You may even start going every day. Your life is changed—for the better—for as long as you maintain the routine.

The same holds true for inbound marketing. You may not see results after that first week. However, if you create content and participate in social media a few times a week for a few months, you will start to see results. The routine will become ingrained in your broader marketing process. You can no longer imagine a week without creating content and participating in social media. You may even do it more often. Your marketing is changed—for the better—for as long as you maintain the routine.

Commit to the process.

Create a Content Production Process

Every year, I speak to many audiences on the aforementioned concepts of inbound marketing. Afterwards, CEOs approach me. "Mark, I loved the speech. Thanks. I made a note to start blogging twice per week."

I smile, excited that I inspired them, and respond, "I appreciate the kind words. Unfortunately, I bet you won't keep it up."

"What?! But wasn't that the whole idea, Mark? Wasn't the point of your talk to transform my behavior?"

Yes, but CEOs are busy. Executives are busy. Salespeople are busy. They work long hours. Their time is in demand and they get pulled in many directions. They may get through the first week or two, but then a new priority arises and the content production comes to a halt.

As an executive, don't think about taking on these tasks yourself. Think instead about creating a content production process. Delegate the process to specialists. That is your job here. Building your content production team is not easy. But once you have the team in place, the hard part is over.

Let's go back to our weight loss analogy. You cannot call up your trainer one day and say, "Hey, I can't make it in to the gym today. Could you bang out a workout for me?" That doesn't work. However, you can get some help with your content production.

There is one key resource of the content production process—*the journalist.* Journalists hold the keys to the future of demand generation! Nobody recognizes this opportunity, not even the journalists themselves. Take advantage. Your job as an executive is to develop this journalistic capability within your company to drive the modern demand generation process.

This can be tricky. Developing this journalistic capability is the hardest, but most important, part of your journey. There are a number of options here. On one end of the spectrum, you could hire a full-time journalist. The good news for you is that many journalists are extraordinarily gifted and, unfortunately, their traditional professional opportunities are become scarcer every day. Newspapers and magazines are on life support. Exceptional journalists are struggling to find work. Find them and hire them.

On the other end of the spectrum, you could hire an intern. Go down to the university near your office with the best journalism program, find a great student, and have them come by your office for a half day every Friday morning to write. If you are extraordinarily budget conscious, you may even be able to pay them through course credit.

Of course, there are many options in between these two extremes. The journalism industry is very open to freelance lifestyles. You can find a freelancer to write for you. Alternatively, do you have an office administrator? Traditionally, these folks have exceptional written communication skills. Could you eliminate a mundane five-hour task in their week to free up time for valuable content production time?

When hiring this journalist, do not obsess about domain experience. This hire does not need to have deep knowledge of your product, your industry, or your buyer. It is helpful, but it is less important than great journalism skills. A great journalist can sit down with a PhD neuroscientist, pick her brain for an hour, and write a beautifully interesting piece of content. They do not need to be experts in the space.

Once you have found the journalist, the next step is to form a thought leadership committee. The thought leadership committee provides the journalist with a continual source of domain knowledge. Anyone at the company who understands your industry, your product value proposition, and your customer's needs should be considered for the thought leadership committee. Certainly your executive team should participate. If you sell a technical product, some engineers should be involved. If you have relationships with partners or external thought leaders, they can contribute as well. Your salespeople on the front lines are valuable resources here because they understand your buyers. They hear the questions buyers have at the beginning of their buying journey. Salespeople have well-rehearsed answers to those questions. They understand which answers resonate with the buyer. These questions and corresponding answers make for beautiful blog articles. In fact, check the "Sent Items" folders on your salespeople's email server. Salespeople often send the same canned responses to their prospects as they address questions that arise throughout the buying journey. These canned emails make for exceptional blog articles.

With both the journalist and thought leadership committee in place, the final step is to put the two functions together to produce content on a continual basis. I refer to this step as defining the content production process. Let's assume you have 10 people on your thought leadership committee. An example content production process would look like this. Every Tuesday at 9 a.m., one member of the thought leadership committee will sit down with the journalist for a one-hour interview. The interview should be on a niche subject. Don't choose your product as the subject. The interview should be about a trend in the industry, a question buyers have early in their buying journey, a phrase that likely resonates with an individual your business can help, and so forth. After this one-hour interview, that member of the thought leadership committee is done for 10 weeks, as the other members will cycle in.

An hour interview can generate a lot of content. From that one-hour interview, the journalist can write a three- to five-page ebook on the discussion topic. The journalist can write three or four short blog posts around niche subjects in the ebook. The journalist can generate dozens of social media messages for Twitter, LinkedIn, and Facebook about the quotes, stats, and trends mentioned in each blog article. Although this content is created within a day or two, it can be scheduled for release to the public over an entire month. Each day of the month, one of the social media messages is published. It links to the corresponding blog article, driving interested readers to the blog. At the end of the blog article is a call to action to the reader that states, "Did you like this blog article on XYZ? Perhaps you will like the ebook we published on the same subject." Many readers click the call to action and are brought to a landing page, where they find out that the ebook is free. They simply need to provide their name, email, phone number, and company URL, and they will have access to the ebook immediately.

This process can be repeated each week. If you're feeling enthusiastic, you can repeat it twice per week or even every day. The result is a stream of high-quality content, developed with minimal budget and minimal time from the executive team and other high-value employees. You have now extracted the brain power of the company and promoted it to your buyers on the digital page. As more and more content is published, more and more potential buyers follow your business on social media. More and more people link to your corporate website and blog. As we learned earlier in this chapter, this rise in social media following and inbound links drives exponential growth in the number of buyers finding you via Google searches. Thanks to the landing page and free ebook offer, a high percentage of these website visitors self-identify themselves to your business in exchange for the complimentary content. This is inbound marketing at its best. This is a formula for predictable, scalable demand generation.

Let's walk through a "before-and-after" example to understand how impactful this demand generation strategy can be. Assume you have 10,000 visitors per month to your website. Let's also assume you have one call to action on your website—"Contact Us." As a result, the website converts only 0.5 percent of your visitors into leads, or 50 leads per month. This is a very common reality for a small or medium-sized business.

"Do not overburden valuable resources at your company with inbound marketing responsibilities. Hire a journalist. Form a thought leadership committee. Put the two together to create a continuous stream of high-quality content."

Now, let's assume you embrace the inbound marketing tactics for a few months. It is not uncommon for traffic to grow by multiples—let's assume three times. Now you are getting 30,000 visitors per month. It is also not uncommon for the visitor-to-lead conversion rate to increase from 0.5 percent to 3 percent with all of these useful ebook offers. At a 3 percent visitor-to-lead conversion rate and 30,000 visitors per month, you are now producing 900 leads per month, up from 50! That represents a "game-changing" impact to your business.

Complement Content Production with Social Media Participation

The content production process is powerful. However, its impact can be significantly amplified by complementing content production with frequent participation in the online discussions where your target buyers are already conversing. Your target buyers are having hundreds, sometimes thousands of conversations online every day. Many of these conversations are related to the value your business provides to these target buyers. Social media is like a live conference that is happening every second of every day. Set up your booth and get involved in the conversation.

Here are some examples of the nooks in which your target buyers may be conversing, and examples of how you can engage with them online.

Perhaps there are a handful of blogs that many of your target buyers read. You should read those blogs too. Add value to the conversation by leaving an intelligent comment. Sign the comment with your name and hyperlink your name back to your blog. If you leave the first comment on a hot article that eventually goes viral, that will be more beneficial than any online advertisement you can purchase. Furthermore, most great bloggers love getting comments on their blogs. They often respond to the comments. They mentally note who leaves insightful comments on their blogs. Don't be afraid to reach out to them via email once you have been active on their blog for some time. Form a tighter relationship with the blogger. Invite them to guest blog on your blog. Ask if you can submit a guest blog for their blog. They will probably be interested. Now your thought leadership will be promoted to a new audience of target customers.

Even better, your thought leadership gets a big rubber stamp of approval because this blogger, whom the audience already trusts, has authorized and endorsed your content. How valuable will that be to you?

Another source you may try is Twitter. Find the people on Twitter who your target buyers follow. Follow these same Twitter users. Read their tweets. Retweet the posts you find interesting and relevant to your buyers. A lot of these authoritative Twitter users will probably follow you back. Don't be afraid to reach out to them via email and form a tighter relationship with them, just as you did with the bloggers. The next time you publish a piece of content, ask if they wouldn't mind promoting it on their Twitter stream. If you have already scratched their back by promoting their stuff a few times, and if your content is high-quality, almost all of them will return the favor. Now their 5,000 followers, the majority of whom are target customers for you, just received a big stamp of approval for your thought leadership (and your business) from a thought leader they trust. How valuable will that be to you?

Finally, find the LinkedIn groups in which your prospects are congregating. Read the questions they ask. Answer the questions that are most relevant to your company's value proposition. Don't worry about promoting your product. In fact, don't mention it. Don't even worry about promoting your content. Simply answer their questions with smart responses. Add value. Be helpful. Show off how knowledgeable you are in the space. People will click through your response to your LinkedIn profile. They will notice the company you work for. They will probably check it out. They will probably read your content and subscribe to it. How valuable will that be to you?

Social media participation is not a one-way stream to promote your content. That is an egotistical approach. That is too selfish. That is not networking. The best networkers at an event don't show up and just talk about themselves. They meet people. They ask questions. They add value. Use these same techniques online. As a rule of thumb,

I like one-third of my social media messages to be about my company and two-thirds to be about other people.

Long-Tail Theory

There is an important concept that was created over a decade ago by Christopher Anderson in his book, *The Long Tail*. The long tail refers to the fact that, within a given population, a large percentage of overall data will be represented by the multitude of small data batches scattered farther down the curve. This concept is important for successful inbound marketing, especially as it relates to selecting content topics.

Figure 10.1 illustrates the long-tail concept.

Let's add some context to this chart. Let's assume the chart is illustrating various books sold in this year. In this case, the x-axis, labeled "Products," would represent the titles of all the books that will be sold this year. The y-axis, labeled "Popularity," represents the total sales for each book. The best seller of the year is listed first and all the other titles, listed in order of total sales, follow along the x-axis. At the

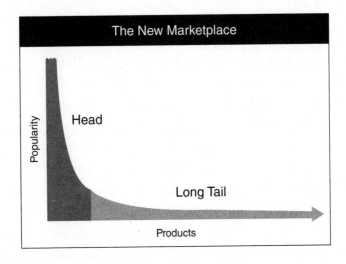

Figure 10.1   The Long-Tail Theory

extreme right of the x-axis are the many titles that will sell only a handful of copies this year. The first books listed have generated enormous revenues. The area under the curve represents the total revenue generated by all of the books produced this year.

By segmenting this revenue, we can illustrate the long-tail concept. The area under the "head" of the curve represents the revenue generated from the best sellers of the year. This is where brick-and-mortar book stores had to make their money. Because of the limitations on physical inventory in their stores, it only made sense for them to sell the absolute best-selling books. These businesses are limited to the revenue potential illustrated at the "head" of the curve.

As a reader, if I wanted to purchase a book written many years ago that is no longer a best seller, I certainly would not stroll down to my local bookstore. The book likely wouldn't be in stock. Where would I go? Amazon.com, of course. One way Amazon.com differentiated itself, especially in its early years, was by doing business in the "long-tail" area of the curve. In many industries, the area under the tail is actually greater than the area under the head. Most importantly, it is often less competitive. The Internet enables businesses to attract customers by using the "long-tail" portion of the curve. The "long-tail" concept can be applied to the movie rental business, with Netflix versus Blockbuster. It can be applied to video content, with YouTube versus cable TV. It can be applied to music, with Spotify versus Best Buy.

So how does long-tail theory apply to your business? As you embark on a content product process, focus on the "long tail," not on the "head," especially when selecting target topics. If you sell IT services, don't focus on phrases like "IT consultant" or "information technology." These words sit at the head of the curve. Yes, there are millions of searches per month. However, it is extraordinarily competitive to rank for these terms. Furthermore, a small portion of the visitors are actually qualified buyers for your business. Instead, focus on "Sharepoint implementations" or "IT for pharmaceutical companies" or "hosted VOIP implementations." There are not millions of searches for these terms every month. However, there are still hundreds of them, and the people searching for these terms are much more qualified for your business than those folks searching for the generic, far more competitive phrases. Each piece of content you produce targets a different slice of the long tail. Each piece of content attracts hundreds of highly qual-

ified buyers to your business. The more you publish content along this strategy, the larger the portion of the long tail you can own. As we stated earlier, the long tail can often be more valuable than the head.

> *Focus your content on "long-tail" topics. They are less competitive and more likely to attract your target buyer.*

This chapter introduces the basics of inbound marketing to modernize your demand generation strategy. For a deeper dive into this concept, read *Inbound Marketing*, by the HubSpot co-founders Brian Halligan and Dharmesh Shah.

To Recap

- Today's buyer is empowered by the Internet. A modern demand generation strategy means less focus on interruptive outbound marketing and more focus on inbound marketing.
- Successful inbound marketing comes from two tactics: (1) continual quality content production, and (2) frequent online participation in social media where your target buyers are already conversing.
- Do not overburden valuable resources at your company with inbound marketing responsibilities. Hire a journalist. Form a thought leadership committee. Put the two together to create a continuous stream of high-quality content.
- Focus your content on "long-tail" topics. They are less competitive and more likely to attract your target buyer.

11

Converting Inbound Interest into Revenue

At least five times per month, I would receive the following email from one of our account managers at HubSpot:

> Mark,
>
> I could use your help with one of our customers. The customer signed up for HubSpot six months ago. They are doing great with their inbound marketing. When the customer signed up, they were getting a few dozen leads through their website per month. Now they are getting over 500 leads per month!
>
> Here is the issue. The salespeople hate the leads. They believe the lead quality is really low. Would you mind jumping on a call with their head of marketing and their head of sales to help figure out the issue?

Of course I was willing to help. Every time I did, I found the same set of issues. Some of the issues were caused by the manner in which

127

marketing was handling the leads. Some of the issues were caused by the manner in which sales was handling the leads. I will elaborate on both sets of issues in this chapter.

Marketing's Role in Converting Interest into Revenue

The Internet has empowered buyers. In many cases, the first few stages of the buying journey happen online. As such, marketing is playing an ever increasing role in the selling process, nurturing these prospects and passing them to sales at precisely the right time.

Here are the most common mistakes and the most important best practices marketing needs to adopt as they work with sales to convert interest into revenue.

The Most Common Mistake: Don't Pass All the Leads to Sales

Imagine for a moment that you're the head of marketing at the company described at the beginning of this chapter. In a span of six months, you have increased the number of leads generated through your firm's website from a few dozen per month to 500 per month. You are a hero! You are going to drive your company to the next level of success. Your instinctive reaction is to get these leads into the hand of the sales team as soon as possible so that the sales team can turn the leads into customers and revenue.

There is one problem. Not all of these inbound leads are qualified for the business. In fact, the majority are not. Let's appreciate the difference between an inbound-generated lead and an outbound-generated lead. Figure 11.1 helps us appreciate this difference.

Outbound sales is represented by the graphic on the left. Outbound sales campaigns start with a list of leads that are presumably a good "fit" for the business. If the company targets the Fortune 5000

Figure 11.1 Outbound Sales vs. Inbound Sales

telecom industry, the company purchases a list of CEOs from the Fortune 5000 telecom industry. Then, Sales and Marketing go to work on that list as aggressively as possible with direct mail, email spam, targeted advertising, and cold calls hoping that 1 percent of the purchased leads respond to these forms of interruptive, outbound selling. The leads that indeed respond probably have some form of "pain", which triggers the response.

Inbound selling is represented by the graphic on the right. The inbound graphic is an inverse representation of the outbound graphic. Most of the leads generated from inbound marketing have a "pain" that needs to be solved. Why else would they have conducted the Google search, read the blog article, or downloaded the ebook? Unfortunately, not all of the inbound leads are a good "fit." Some of the leads are perfect prospects, because they are executives from the Fortune 5000 telecom industry. These are beautiful leads. They represent the right person at the right company, and they have a pain that your product can solve. However, some of the leads are not a good fit. Some of the leads are PhD students from Asia, simply doing research for their dissertations. These leads will probably never be buyers of your product.

If some of the inbound leads are not qualified buyers, it does not mean inbound is failing. The situation simply needs to be managed in the right way. Let's get back to our example from the beginning of this chapter, in which the marketing team has used inbound tactics to generate 500 leads per month. Let's take an extreme case and assume that only 10 percent, or 50 of these leads per month, are properly qualified leads. These 50 leads are beautiful leads. The companies are a perfect "fit" because they all have a "pain" that you can solve. These leads will probably close at twice the rate in half the time when compared to your traditional outbound leads. This is a wonderful situation!

Here's the snag: if the marketing team passes all 500 of these inbound leads over to sales, representing the 50 great leads and the 450 weak leads, the sales team will ultimately hate the entire batch. Why? The sales team will need to crawl through 10 leads just to find one solid one, which is a frustrating experience for the salespeople.

Let's improve this process. If the marketing team filters the leads and passes only the 50 great leads to sales, the sales team will think they have the best marketing team on the planet. They will praise marketing. They will beg the executive team to invest more in marketing.

When a company is in the early stages of its inbound marketing journey, the lead filtering process does not need to be sophisticated. In many cases, someone on the marketing team can simply screen the leads and pass the best ones through to sales. In the early stages of inbound marketing, the lead flow is low enough that this manual process is manageable. As lead flow increases, more advanced techniques are needed, which I will address later in this chapter.

Avoid the Lead Scoring Trap

Once marketing teams increase their inbound lead flow volume, they often introduce a lead scoring system. In general, implementing a lead scoring system is a smart move. Unfortunately, lead scoring is often implemented in a manner that causes more harm than good.

Issues arise when the lead scoring algorithm becomes too complicated. This is a common situation. For example, the marketing team may announce, "Once a lead exceeds a lead score of 50, the lead will be passed to sales." In a vacuum, this statement sounds harmless. But what does a score of 50 *mean*? How does the scoring algorithm work?

In many cases, the scoring algorithm is based on an overly complicated set of factors. For example, if the lead provides an email, the lead score increases by two points. If the lead views the pricing page, the lead score increases by seven points. If the lead requests a demo, the lead score increases by 10 points. The act of downloading an ebook increases the score by five points. Additional ebook downloads are two points each. There are so many permutations that could get the lead score above 50, or keep the lead score below 50. How do you know that passing the lead to sales precisely when the lead score exceeds 50 is the right move in all cases? Depending on how the lead score is set up, a start-up intern who downloads 20 ebooks on a Saturday night might get passed to sales, while an important individual who visits one page and requests a demo (but takes no further action) might not.

At HubSpot, we tried the lead scoring approach, but ran into the problems I just described. We evolved to implement an alternative approach we called the "Buyer Persona/Buyer Journey" matrix, or buyer matrix for short. Figure 11.2 shows an example of a buyer matrix.

The vertical axis (*y*-axis) shows the different buyer personas the company targets. Buyer personas are defined by primarily static

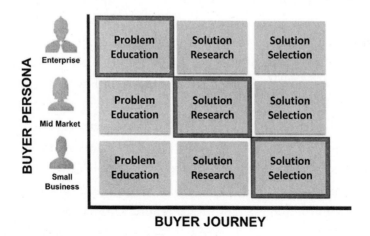

Figure 11.2   Buyer Persona/Buyer Journey Matrix

attributes about the buyer that will not change. Example attributes include the size of the business, the industry of the company, the role of the buyer, and so forth. In the example in Figure 11.2, we are targeting three buyer personas: Small Business, Mid-Market, and Enterprise.

The horizontal axis (*x*-axis) shows the different stages through which the buyer progresses during the buyer journey. These stages of the buyer will likely change, hopefully as quickly as possible. In this example, we have three stages of the buyer journey: Problem Education, Solution Research, and Solution Selection.

With the buyer personas and the buyer journey defined, our example buyer matrix is established! The three-by-three matrix yields nine unique "buyer states," with each buyer state representing a specific buyer persona at a specific stage in the buying journey. We are now in a position to customize the experience that each buyer has with our company based on who they are and where they are in the process. We can customize our marketing, our sales, our product, and our customer support to match their buyer state.

As an example, assume a potential buyer is in the "Small Business/ Problem Education" buyer state. We should strive to customize her entire experience with our company based on her buyer state. When this buyer visits our website, she should be greeted with a call to action to download an ebook on small business marketing trends in 2014. If the sales team connects with this buyer, the sales team should reference educational collateral we developed for buyers early in their buying journey.

On the other hand, if we are dealing with a potential buyer in the "Small Business/Solution Selection" buyer state, the call to action on the website should be to read a case study about a small business customer in his industry. When the sales team engages with this buyer, the sales team should reference ROI reports summarizing our similar customers' success with our products. The prospective buyer's experience with the entire company is optimized for that buyer's state.

When you first set up the matrix, do not feel pressure to create a highly customized, thoroughly tested experience for each buyer state right away. Instead, implement something basic for each box. Use your gut. Form some theories.

Once the basic theories are in place, make sure you have a way to measure the performance of the tactics within each buyer state. How many buyers enter each buyer state every month? How many buyers move on in their journey? How many buyers get stuck or exit the funnel? Where do they get stuck and after how long?

A disciplined measurement strategy for the buyer matrix allows you to analyze, test, and optimize the entire matrix, one buyer state at a time. Take a step back and decide which buyer states are performing poorly and represent the best opportunities for improvement. Pick one. Analyze the performance of that buyer state. Take a deep look at buyers who are progressing quickly through it. What content did they consume? What actions did they take? What actions did your company take to accelerate them through that state? Then take a deep look at buyers who are stuck in that buyer state. Don't be afraid to call them to diagnose the blockers that are preventing them from progressing in their buyer journey. Form theories on how to resolve the issues. Run some experiments. Optimize and improve. Then move on to the next buyer state.

Use the Buyer Matrix to Determine When to Pass Leads to Sales

With a well-formed buyer matrix in place, let's get back to the original question. When should each type of lead be passed to sales? Let's address this question within the context of the matrix.

Start with a theory for each persona. Assume we want to pass the "Enterprise" persona leads to sales at the first stage of their journey, the "Problem Education" stage. Our gut tells us that Enterprise opportunities have sizeable revenue potential. If an employee at a

Fortune 500 company even touches our website, subscribes to our blog, or mentions us in social media, we probably want a salesperson to follow up immediately.

For the "Mid-Market" persona, assume we want to pass the leads to sales at the "Solution Research" stage. These mid-market companies probably do not have quite as much revenue upside as the Enterprise customers. Marketing will nurture these buyers through the Problem Education stage. Once the buyer's actions suggest he has reached the Solution Research stage (perhaps he downloaded product information or requested a product demonstration), the buyer will be passed to a salesperson.

For the "Small Business" persona, let's assume we want to pass the leads to sales at the "Solution Selection" stage. These small businesses have a limited budget and, in turn, limited revenue potential. However, there are *a lot* of them. Marketing will nurture these buyers through both the Problem Education and Solution Research stages. Once the buyers indicate they are at the Solution Selection stage (perhaps they are actively using the free trial product), they will be passed to a salesperson.

Once your theory is in place, start funneling leads to Sales according to the proposed plan and measure lead conversion success. If lead conversion is remarkably low for a given buyer persona, consider moving the "pass to Sales" threshold to the right in the matrix. Require Marketing to nurture the buyers further before passing them to Sales. If the lead conversion is remarkably high for a given buyer persona, consider moving the "pass to Sales" threshold to the left in the matrix. Pass the lead to Sales sooner!

Figure 11.3 illustrates the lead conversion progress for each buyer persona in our example.

In this example, this analysis is conducted at the end of Q3, based on all of the leads generated in Q1. As a result, these leads have had sufficient time to work themselves through the buyer journey.

Let's take a look at the Enterprise segment. A total of 1,500 new leads reached the Problem Education stage and were immediately

	Leads Passed to Sales	Lead-to-Customer %	Customers	Total Revenue	Revenue per Customer
Enterprise	1,500	3%	45	$31.5M	$700K
Mid Market	7,000	6%	420	$84M	$200K
Small Business	11,000	20%	2,200	$88M	$40K

BUYER PERSONA

FUNNEL PERFORMANCE

Figure 11.3 Analyzing When to Pass Leads to Sales

passed to the sales team in Q1. By the end of Q3, 3 percent of those leads had converted to customers, for a total of 45 customers. The average annual contract size for each of these customers was $700,000.

In the Mid-Market group, 7,000 leads were nurtured to the Solution Education stage and passed to sales in Q1. By the end of Q3, 6 percent of those leads had converted to customers, for a total of 420 customers. The average annual contract size for each of these customers was $200,000.

In the Small Business group, 11,000 leads were nurtured to the Problem Selection stage and passed to sales in Q1. By the end of Q3, 20 percent of those leads had converted to customers, for a total of 2,200 customers. The average annual contract size for each of these customers was $40,000.

With the conversion data in place, we can start to optimize the stage at which each buyer should be passed to sales. For example, one conclusion to draw from this data is that the customer conversion rate on Small Business leads is really high. Perhaps we waited too long to call these leads, and failed to call some closable prospects that hadn't progressed beyond Solution Selection. Obviously, this theory can be tested. Instead of waiting for small business buyers to reach the Solution Selection stage, we can start passing the leads to the sales team when the Small Business buyers reach the Problem Education stage. Let's assume, after running the experiment, we find that 30,000 Small Business leads were nurtured to the Problem Education stage and passed to the sales team. After a few quarters, only 5 percent of those leads converted to customers, for a total of 1,500 customers. The average purchase price remained the same at $40,000.

In this case, the experiment failed. When the Small Business leads were passed to Sales at the Solution Selection stage, the small business sales team converted 2,200 customers at an average purchase price of $40,000. They generated $88 million from those leads. During the experiment, the Small Business leads were sent to the sales team at the Problem Education stage. The sales team converted 1,500 customers at an average purchase price of $40,000. They generated $60 million from those leads. The team performed better when the leads were passed to Sales at the Solution Selection stage. When the leads were passed at the Problem Education stage, the team was likely overwhelmed with the volume of leads and wasted more time on lesser qualified opportunities. This, in turn, drove down revenue productivity.

Become a Buyer Matrix Expert through Microsegmentation

In this example, we started with a very simple buyer matrix. I recommend you do the same when starting out. However, as you begin to understand your buyer matrix in greater detail, you realize that there are more complex behaviors in play than this simple model can accommodate. For example, in the Enterprise segment, there are typically multiple individuals involved in the buyer journey. Each of these individuals has unique interests. Finance, marketing, and IT may all have influence over the decision. How do we account for all of these influences in the buyer matrix? In the Small Business segment, you may sell to multiple industries, such as technology, finance, and health care. Each industry has unique perspectives throughout the buyer journey. How do we account for these different industries in the buyer matrix?

As you become more of an expert with your buyer matrix, you can introduce microsegments to address these complications. Let's use the multi-influencer Enterprise example described earlier. Take the entire Enterprise row and create a new matrix for this row. This time the y-axis reflects the different influencer roles, such as marketing end user, IT, and finance. We'll keep the buyer journey the same. Now I can further customize the individual's experience with my company. As such, I may show different sets of content to the IT manager and the marketing end user, all adjusted to the stage they are at in their journey.

Sales' Role in Converting Interest into Revenue

Just like Marketing, Sales needs to evolve its strategy when handling inbound leads.

Any difficulties that salespeople have adjusting to these inbound leads usually stem from the fact that some of the classic training that salespeople have received over the past few decades does not apply when working with inbound leads. In fact, these legacy tactics can actually hurt the sale. There are three specific aspects of legacy selling that hurt inbound lead handling the most.

Scrap the Elevator Pitch—Lead with Context

Has your name ever been on a salesperson's call list? Did you receive a lot of voicemails from that salesperson over the course of a few weeks?

Think back to those voicemails. Were they valuable? Did you learn anything that helped you? Or were the voicemails a carbon copy of the company's elevator pitch?

I probably receive about 20 cold calls a day from various salespeople. Here is an example call sequence I receive from a salesperson.

[Tuesday at 9 a.m.] "Hi, Mark. This is John from XYZ Company. Would you like to reach more decision makers with your sales team's calling efforts? Our company can deliver the names and contact information for thousands of decision makers at Fortune 500 companies. We have state-of-the-art technology that maximizes the accuracy of our data. Please reach out to me today so I can show you some sample lists."

[Thursday at 8 a.m.] "Hi, Mark. This is John again from XYZ Company. Would you like to reach more decision makers with your sales team's calling efforts? Our company can deliver the names and contact information for thousands of decision makers at Fortune 500 companies. We have state-of-the-art technology that maximizes the accuracy of our data. Please reach out to me today so I can show you some sample lists."

[Monday at 10 a.m.] "Hi, Mark. John over here at XYZ Company. You probably remember that we can deliver the names and contact information for thousands of decision makers at Fortune 500 companies. We have state-of-the-art technology that maximizes the accuracy of our data. I would love to show you these names. Call me today when you have a second."

Torture!

It is hard to listen to this stuff. I can't imagine being on the other side of the phone, leaving this monotony of voicemails every day.

Not only is this approach inappropriate in any modern prospecting situation, it is also the kiss of death for an inbound lead. Your marketing team has invested significant amounts of time and money to attract this buyer, using quality educational content that is highly relevant to the buyer's context. The buyer has had a great experience perusing the articles on your blog, reading through ebooks, and attending webinars that your company has produced to help them frame their problem better. When thinking about the problems the buyer is looking to solve, the buyer perceives your company as smart, helpful, and relevant.

Then a classically trained salesperson calls the prospect and leaves one of the voicemails listed earlier.

Disaster! Insert explosion sounds here. All of marketing's effective inbound work is thrown out the window.

Here is what a HubSpot salesperson's voicemail sequence sounds like:

[Tuesday at 9 a.m.] "Hi, John. This is Mark from HubSpot. I noticed you downloaded our ebook on Facebook marketing best practices. I took a look at your company's Facebook page and had a few suggestions for improving it. I'll email those to you now. Give me a call if you want to discuss."

[Thursday at 3 p.m.] "Hi, John. Mark again from HubSpot. Great news! I found a customer of ours in your industry who had enormous success with their Facebook marketing strategy. I am going to send you that case study now to give you an idea of the specific tactics they used and the results you should expect. Give me a call if you would like to review it together."

[Monday at 12 p.m.] "Hi, John. Mark at HubSpot. I actually ran that customer of ours in your industry through our Marketing Grader tool and compared their presence on social media to yours. They scored an 87. You scored a 54. I am going to send you those reports now. It turns out there is a lot more opportunity outside of Facebook in the broader social media area for you. Call me if you want to walk through the report."

And so on . . .

Compare this buyer context–oriented approach to the traditional stream of elevator pitches. With which salesperson would you rather engage? The buyer context sales approach is in perfect alignment with the experience the prospective buyer has had with the company thus far. It is educational. It is insightful. It is personalized to his context. It makes engaging with the salesperson feel like the right next step for the prospect to take.

As the salesperson attempts to connect with the buyer through a sequence of voicemails and emails, the salesperson should treat the process like a dialogue. Even though buyers do not always call back, they are usually listening. Add new information into each voicemail. Align the voicemails with the specific interactions the buyers have had with your company.

I will admit that we had a unique advantage at HubSpot when it came to this type of contextual prospecting. The pain points of our prospects were public information. We knew the extent of each prospect's social media presence, their rankings in search engine results, and the effectiveness of their company blog, all without ever speaking with the prospect. Not all sales teams have that luxury.

That doesn't mean you can't use this contextual approach to prospecting. Understand your prospects' context by reviewing the way they found you, the blog article they read, the ebooks they downloaded. From these actions, the salesperson can infer the prospects' specific interests. Share content related to these interests. Tailor the content to the size of their business, their industry, or their role. Instead of suggesting the next step be a demo of your product, suggest a free consultation on whatever topic will pique their interest. Ask one of your internal experts to help. Send your expert's bio to the prospect and offer to connect them on a call. There is so much opportunity to engage with the prospect in a contextual way.

Now, there is a critical element of the modern voicemail sequence that has its roots in traditional, old-school selling strategy. I need to tip my hat to my dad, Rick Roberge, for introducing me to it. Regardless of whether you are coaching your salespeople to leave three voicemails or 12 voicemails, the final message should always be the "going negative" voicemail.

"Hi, John. Mark at HubSpot. I left you a few voicemails with suggestions and best practices on Facebook marketing. I have not heard back from you. I am going to assume that Facebook marketing is no longer a priority for you this year. Give me a call if it ever becomes a priority again."

For whatever reason, the "going negative" voicemail has the highest callback rate. There must be a psychological phenomenon at work here. In any case, if you have done a good job adding value through the contextual prospecting process, the prospect will likely call you back after this voicemail. You have been providing such great information to them. Why would they want the relationship to end?

[Potential Buyer] "Mark. I am so sorry I have not had a chance to call. It has been crazy over here. The information you have sent me is so helpful. Can you chat at noon tomorrow?"

[Salesperson] "Actually, I am tied up. But, I am free at 2 p.m. Does that work?"

[Potential Buyer] "I do have a meeting scheduled, but you know what? I think I can move it. If you are free at 2 p.m., let's chat then."

Call Low, Then Call High

"Call high with the elevator pitch."

That is how a classically trained salesperson approaches cold calling. Find a decision maker. Call with an elevator pitch that would resonate with a decision maker. Perhaps the elevator pitch highlights increased profit margin, or accelerated growth, or decreased COGS.

Now this classically trained salesperson receives her first inbound lead. The lead is from a company that is a perfect fit for the salesperson's product, but the contact is not a decision maker. The contact is a middle manager, or a frontline worker, or even an intern. Unfortunately, the classically trained salesperson does not alter her approach. She calls the contact and leads with her generic elevator pitch—the elevator pitch designed for the decision maker.

This approach is the kiss of death for an inbound lead. Here is what it sounds like:

[Salesperson] "Hi, John. This is Susie from XYZ Company. Do you have a moment?"

[John the Intern] "I guess."

[Salesperson] "Great. John, we have state-of-the-art technology that helps companies like yours decrease COGS by an average of 20 percent and increase profit margins accordingly. I would love an opportunity to show you how we have done this. Would you be free tomorrow for a chat?"

[John the Intern] "Huh?"

The classically trained salesperson hangs up the phone, yelling to her teammates, "These leads suck."

No, they don't. The salesperson is simply approaching the lead incorrectly.

The company is a perfect fit for the business, but the initial contact is not a decision maker. The initial contact is an intern.

So what?

Why do you think the intern is doing this research? A decision maker probably told the intern to do the research because the related problem is important to the business *right now*! So, this means your product can solve an issue that is top of mind for a decision maker. Let's engage in the right way.

There are two strategies the salesperson can take. One strategy is to ignore the initial contact from the inbound lead and instead call the decision maker directly.

"Hi, Mary. This is Mark from HubSpot. We have been receiving a number of inquiries from your team about generating leads through social media. I actually reviewed your Facebook page and had some ideas on how it can be a better lead generator for you. I will send those to you now over email. Call me if you would like to discuss."

In this example, we leveraged the buyer context from the initial contact and assumed the decision maker had a similar context. It is a reasonable bet.

The alternative strategy, which I prefer, is to call the contact from the lead first and then call the decision maker as a follow-up. I call this strategy "call low, then call high." When the salesperson calls the contact from the lead, the salesperson needs to engage the contact with a relevant value proposition, which is not necessarily the most appropriate value proposition for the decision maker.

"Hi, John. This is Mark from HubSpot. I noticed you downloaded our ebook on Facebook marketing lead generation. What specific questions did you have?"

This approach frames the conversation around the topics the inbound lead contact cares about. Give the prospect as many free tips and as much free consulting as possible. With each back and forth, the salesperson is developing trust with the prospect. The salesperson is earning the right to ask questions about the needs of the organization and where those needs are originating—for example:

1. Why did you decide to research the topic of generating leads through Facebook?
2. Was there someone at the company who instructed you to do so?
3. Who do you report to? What have they been asking of you lately?

4. What is on your CEO's mind these days? What did she talk about at the last company meeting?
5. Can you tell me more about your CMO's areas of focus?

If the salesperson is skilled at this approach, she can be quite successful at transforming the inbound lead contact into a "coach." Do not confuse a "coach" with a "champion." In most cases, the inbound lead contact does not have enough authority to be considered a "champion." In other words, the inbound prospect can't influence the organization enough to compel the purchase. However, as a "coach," the prospect can be useful to provide internal context about the opportunity so that the salesperson is enabled to help the organization more effectively.

Once the interaction with the inbound prospect is completed, the salesperson can now call high to the decision maker.

"Hi, John. This is Mark from HubSpot. I have been working with members of your team on the company's Facebook lead generation strategy. I am aware that the company has recently decided to expand the sales team by 20 percent in Q4 and is working aggressively to identify new sources of qualified leads to provide to the newest members of the sales team. One of our customers in your industry has had great success with generating leads through social media and actually far exceeded the 20 percent lift you are targeting. Would you have a few minutes to walk through the details of their successful strategy?"

Decision makers are busy. They are hard to reach. However, this voicemail maximizes the likelihood that the salesperson can earn some of the decision maker's time.

Prioritize Prospecting by Level of Engagement, Not Alphabetical Order

Grab one of your salespeople today and ask, "Sally, when you come into the office in the morning and start prospecting, how do you decide who to call first?"

If the answer is, "I sort my leads by alphabetical order," that is not a good sign.

Unfortunately, calling leads in alphabetical order is common at many organizations.

In some cases, the company has a more sophisticated approach and calls the leads on a certain cadence. For example, if company ABC is due for a call today based on when it was last touched, it will automatically be listed in the appropriate salesperson's call queue. This approach is effective in ensuring no leads fall through the cracks, but there are always exceptions.

Pop quiz: here are two leads that your salesperson could call next. Which lead do you think he should prioritize?

1. A lead that was called yesterday, but just visited your company's website two minutes ago
2. A lead that was called three days ago and is now overdue for a follow-up

Pretty obvious—call the first one . . . and do it quickly!

The engagement of the lead is the best criteria around which to prioritize prospecting calls. Unfortunately, few sales teams take this approach. As your marketing department attracts more prospects to your company's online presence, your salespeople need to be equipped with access to the details of each prospect's engagement so they can act on the information. Examples of prospect engagement include:

1. A lead visited my website
2. A lead opened my sales email
3. A lead opened an email from my drip marketing campaign
4. A lead mentioned a key phrase relevant to my business on social media
5. A lead mentioned our company or our competition on social media
6. A lead followed our CEO on Twitter
7. A lead downloaded one of our ebooks

Salespeople need to know in real time when these engagements are occurring, and should be organizing their prospecting activity accordingly. Forget alphabetical order and deprioritize touch cadences.

Specialize Sales by Inbound versus Outbound

As we have discussed in this chapter, selling to an inbound lead requires a new set of skills. For this reason, specializing the members of your sales team by the types of leads they cover (inbound versus outbound) is a good idea. This specialization is also important for another reason: if a salesperson receives 50 inbound leads per month and is asked to supplement his pipeline with cold calling, that salesperson will not do the cold calls. Salespeople will always look for the path of least resistance to hit their goal. If you do not give a salesperson any inbound leads and tell them they need to hit quota through cold calling, they'll find a way to make it happen.

This is the approach we used at HubSpot as we scaled to $100M in revenue. We had one team that called the inbound leads exclusively. They got really good at using specific tactics to engage with these inbound leads. We got really good at sizing this team in order to optimize the lead flow per salesperson and the time spent on each lead. We had another team that had to get to goal by cold calling. These folks were given business development reps, or BDRs, who made the cold calls and set appointments for the outbound closing specialists. This team could take advantage of targeting perfect-fit companies but had the added task of educating cold prospects and creating pain points.

This tactic of specializing by lead source works really well during the $0 to $100 million journey. I have seen it implemented at many start-ups, and it immediately resolves issues of salespeople refusing to call inbound leads or refusing to make cold calls. In most cases, companies are transitioning from a small team that exclusively makes cold calls to a hybrid structure that accommodates inbound volume. The best thing to do is take your top-performing salespeople and rotate the inbound leads between them. That way, they can start developing the inbound-oriented tactical skills that work best. You can start to experiment with the right lead volume per salesperson and start scaling that team accordingly.

The one pitfall you need to avoid is the excuse from the inbound team that they can't hit their goal because the marketing department is not delivering. Even the inbound team needs to be empowered to hit their goal regardless of marketing's performance. There are a few ways to do this:

1. Keep closers as generalists and specialize only the appointment setters by inbound versus outbound strategy. The closing salespeople deal with all opportunities generated, and can allocate their time based on where they (and their appointment setters) are seeing the most action.
2. Provide each inbound salesperson with a set of named accounts that they can work in addition to the inbound demand that is coming in.

To Recap, when implementing an inbound sales and marketing revenue machine

Marketing needs to:

1. Filter the leads. Avoid passing all inbound leads to Sales.
2. Avoid the lead scoring trap. Use a Buyer Persona/Buyer Journey matrix to decide when to pass leads to Sales.

Sales needs to:

1. Call low, and then call high. On the call, scrap the generic elevator pitch.
2. Prioritize prospecting by engagement, not call cadence or alphabetical order.
3. Consider specializing the team by inbound or outbound.

12 | Aligning Sales and Marketing—The SMarketing SLA

Here is an outrageous overgeneralization:

"Traditionally, Sales teams and Marketing teams have not always gotten along with each other."

You would be amazed at the laughs, smirks, and head nodding that I observe when I make this statement in front of an audience.

It's true.

For many organizations, the relationship between Sales and Marketing is dysfunctional. Marketing sits in one corner of the office, harboring the perception that the sales team is a group of overpaid, self-centered brats who fail to see the big-picture strategy. Sales is in another corner of the office, thinking that the marketing team sits around doing arts and crafts all day and has no idea what a qualified lead looks like. Rather than working together, these two teams retreat to their respective corners, with Sales cranking out their cold calls and Marketing working on trade shows and corporate branding exercises.

> *"The dysfunctional relationship between Sales and Marketing is the kiss of death in a buyer-driven world."*

This dysfunctional relationship between Sales and Marketing is the kiss of death in a buyer-driven world. Buyers begin their journey online, conducting research on the problems they are experiencing or the opportunities they would like to pursue. Marketing needs to own this initial stage of engagement, nurture buyers through the initial phases of their journey, and seamlessly pass the buyer to Sales at the most appropriate and helpful time. Sales needs to pick up where Marketing left off, creating continuity in the buyer's experience with the broader organization.

Fortunately for me, our CMO at HubSpot, Mike Volpe, was an amazing partner to me in this journey. My relationship with Mike originated at MIT, years before HubSpot ever existed. We were both quants. We both appreciated the paradigm shift toward a buyer-centric world. We both wanted to scale a big company. We knew it was critical to achieve Sales and Marketing alignment, rather than find ourselves mired in dysfunction.

> *"Use the Sales and Marketing SLA to replace the subjective and qualitative aspects of the Sales/Marketing relationship with well-defined targets and quantified goals."*

Reverting to the quant-oriented lens through which we viewed the world, Mike and I set out to establish a service level agreement, or "SLA," between our two teams. SLAs are commonly established in the world of IT in order to quantify the acceptable availability of a system (e.g., 99.999 percent uptime per month). Our mission with the Sales and Marketing SLA was to establish similarly quantified agreements between the two teams.

The Marketing Service Level Agreement (SLA)

The first step in establishing the Marketing SLA was to define when a lead would be qualified to be passed to the Sales team. This topic was covered thoroughly in Chapter 11. The decision to pass a lead to Sales is best derived from the Buyer Matrix. It depends on the type of company the lead represents and the level of engagement the lead has had with your Sales and Marketing teams thus far.

Referring back to our Buyer Matrix in Chapter 11, we established that leads with a "Mid-Market" buyer persona would be passed to Sales when they reached the "Solution Research" buying journey stage. To add more context to our example, let's assume that a typical Mid-Market lead represents a company with 1,000–10,000 employees. Let's also assume that for a Mid-Market lead to reach the "Solution Research" stage, the lead needs to have downloaded information about our product or requested a demonstration. If Marketing delivers a lead that meets these criteria, the lead "does not suck." Sales should engage with it. If Sales continues to resist these types of leads, then either Sales needs additional training on how to engage these leads or the Marketing SLA needs to be revised to better define what makes a lead worthy of Sales' attention.

With a clear lead quality definition in place, the quantity of leads expected each month needed to be established as well. Mike and I studied the optimal lead flow a bit. For the purpose of this example, let's assume that the optimal number of qualified leads per month for a mid-market salesperson was 150. Let's assume that if a mid-market salesperson was provided with 150 leads per month, the salesperson connected with 50 percent of the leads, created 25 qualified sales opportunities, moved 15 of the opportunities to the presentation stage, and converted five of the presentations into paying customers every month, thus achieving his revenue goals.

Given the assumptions in this example, the Marketing SLA was easy to calculate. If there are 10 salespeople on the mid-market team and each mid-market salesperson needs 150 qualified leads per month, then Mike needed to deliver 1,500 qualified leads each month in order for the team to hit their goal. In my experience, companies that reach this level of precision rank in the top 5 percent of Sales and Marketing alignment excellence.

Unfortunately, Mike and I found that our precise approach was not quite world-class. Here's why: under the foregoing model, if a VP of marketing visited the HubSpot website and filled out a form to download some collateral on our product, that action would generate a qualified lead. Why wouldn't it? It is a great lead! If a different VP of marketing visited the HubSpot website and was active in a trial of our free product, that action would generate a qualified lead as well. It is also a great lead!

Which type of lead do you think closed at a higher rate—the product collateral download or the active free trial? The active free trial closed at a higher rate, of course! This type of lead was further along in the buyer journey. It was at the "Solution Selection" stage of the buyer journey, rather than the "Solution Research" stage. In our case, active free trials closed at many times the rate of product collateral downloads.

Think about the issue a different way: Which lead do you think was easier for Marketing to generate, the product collateral download or the active free trial? The product collateral was easier for Marketing to generate, of course!

Keeping this logic in mind, and referring back to our Marketing SLA of 1,500 qualified leads per month, which type of lead do you think the sales team received more often, product collateral downloads or active free trials? Which "call to action" do you think appeared more frequently on our website, "download product collateral" or "start free trial"? When Marketing fell behind on their SLA and prepared an emergency email to generate some demand, do you think the email campaign focused on product collateral downloads or on free trials? In all cases, the answer was the product collateral downloads.

The teams were not as aligned as we had hoped. The Sales team preferred active free trials. However, the way the SLA was structured, the marketing team was better off focusing on product collateral downloads. As precise as our approach to the Marketing SLA was, it did not account for the fact that different prospect actions reflected different stages of the buyer journey. The process needed to be refined.

To account for the different qualification levels of leads, we focused less on the raw number of leads generated and more on the implied dollar value of leads generated. Here is how we engineered each lead's implied dollar value:

1. For each buyer state, we calculated the average rate at which these leads converted to customers.
2. For each segment, we calculated the average purchase price for each customer generated from these classes of leads.
3. We then multiplied the conversion rate by the average purchase price. This simple arithmetic exercise yielded the dollar value of each lead in that Buyer Persona/Buyer Journey segment.

Figure 12.1 illustrates the conversion rates, purchase prices, and resulting implied lead values for all buyer states established in Chapter 11.

Small Business Persona

Buyer Journey State	Customer Conversion %	Revenue per Customer	Lead Value
Problem Education	1%	$40K	$400
Solution Research	5%	$40K	$2K
Solution Selection	20%	$40K	$8K

Mid-Market Persona

Buyer Journey State	Customer Conversion %	Revenue per Customer	Lead Value
Problem Education	2%	$200K	$4K
Solution Research	6%	$200K	$12K
Solution Selection	25%	$200K	$50K

Enterprise Persona

Buyer Journey State	Customer Conversion %	Revenue per Customer	Lead Value
Problem Education	3%	$700K	$21K
Solution Research	10%	$700K	$70K
Solution Selection	30%	$700K	$210K

Figure 12.1   Foundation for the Marketing SLA

With the implied dollar values of leads established, the Marketing SLA was no longer based on a raw number of leads, but instead on an aggregate implied lead dollar value. For example, the Marketing team did not need to deliver 1,500 mid-market qualified leads to the mid-market sales team. They needed to deliver $12 million of mid-market implied lead value. Marketing could achieve that goal by producing 1,000 demo requests, generating 3,000 product collateral downloads, or producing some appropriate combination of both. Whatever the case, statistically speaking, the Sales team would have enough qualified leads to hit their numbers.

"The Marketing SLA provides a framework to put Marketing on a revenue quota, similar to Sales."

Taking a step back, we essentially put Marketing on a revenue quota! Sales is not the only team accountable to the revenue. Marketing is as well.

The strategy worked beautifully. One week after transitioning to this approach, the focus of the calls to action on the website transitioned from product collateral downloads to free trials. Sales was happy with the improved lead quality. Marketing received proper credit for their hard work. A much deeper degree of alignment had been achieved.

In actuality, our Buyer Matrix was far more granular. There were a multitude of segments with which we were dealing. Nevertheless, this example illustrates the basics of our marketing SLA strategy. Start with high-level segments. As you understand your model, carve up the segments more granularly in order to hone in on the optimal strategy for each slice.

The Sales Service Level Agreement (SLA)

The service level agreement is bidirectional. Cooperation is a two-way street, and Sales must hold up their end of the bargain. If

Marketing is going to hold themselves to a high level of precision, then Sales needs to be on the hook for effectively working the leads generated by Marketing. Sales cannot sit back and say, "More, more, more!"

But what does it mean to "work a lead effectively"?

I pondered this question for many hours. Let's start with a simple question regarding lead follow-up: How soon after the time of lead conversion should the salesperson call the lead?

There is a lot of data in the market that suggests salespeople should work inbound leads within minutes of conversion. I buy into that theory. I have run my own analysis on this theory and validated it within the HubSpot context. A lead that is called within minutes versus hours or days converts to a customer at an exponentially higher rate. Clearly, the span of time within which a salesperson works a newly converted lead should be part of the Sales SLA. For example, one aspect of the Sales SLA could be:

"Every lead from the website should be called within one hour of converting."

Here is another set of questions: If the salesperson calls the lead and gets a voicemail, when should the salesperson try the lead again? Should the salesperson call back that evening, tomorrow, next week? How many times should the salesperson call the lead before he gives up? As a sales leader, should I strive to give each salesperson one lead per month and have the salesperson call that lead a thousand times? Should I prefer to give each salesperson a thousand leads per month and have the salesperson call each lead once?

> *"Sales is accountable to Marketing just like Marketing is accountable to Sales. The Sales SLA defines a series of behaviors expected of the Sales team to ensure each lead is worked effectively."*

Well, as a quant, I studied a lot of these questions. Figure 12.2 is an example of the output that came from these analyses. While the data is

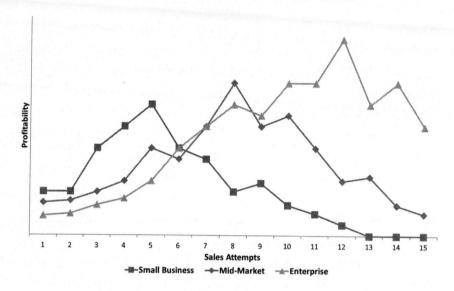

Figure 12.2   The Foundation of the Sales SLA

altered a bit, the end conclusions are similar to the conclusions we drew from the actual analysis.

In this example, 50,000 sales leads are analyzed. Some of those leads were called only once (I wasn't pleased to see this). Some of them were called 12 times. Obviously, if you call a lead more frequently, you are more likely to get someone on the phone. However, it costs you more organizational time to do so. Therefore, what is the right balance between calling more frequently and managing the time invested per lead? The y-axis attempts to answer this question. The y-axis plots the profitability of calling a lead the number of times denoted on the x-axis. Whichever call attempt volume yields the highest profitability is the ideal per-lead call volume we are looking for. In this example, Figure 12.2 illustrates that the optimal number of times to call a small business lead is five. For mid-market leads, the optimal number of call attempts is eight. For enterprise companies, the optimal number of call attempts is twelve.

With this data in hand, I was equipped to guide the team. Holding up the chart to the team, I exclaimed, "Folks, we calculated the ideal call patterns that will lead to you making the most money at HubSpot." [*Applause. Salespeople are coin-operated.*]

"Folks, we programmed these call patterns into the CRM so you do not even have to think about them. The CRM will tell you when to call each lead next." [*Applause. Sales people prefer to think about the hard stuff like breaking the ice and building rapport, not when to time their next call.*]

"Folks, we created a daily dashboard so that none of your leads will slip through the cracks." [*Applause, as long as you have built a data-driven sales culture from the start. Salespeople like having a mechanism to back themselves up.*]

The last point is important. We created a daily report distributed every evening to both the Sales and Marketing teams, holding both organizations accountable for the SLAs established. Figure 12.3 shows the Marketing team's performance against their SLA.

The diamond line plots the ideal lead value generated from the first day of a month to the last day of the month. The square line shows the actual lead value generated each day. The Marketing team tried to keep the actual lead value as close as possible to the ideal lead value. If the actual lead value deviated from the ideal lead value in either

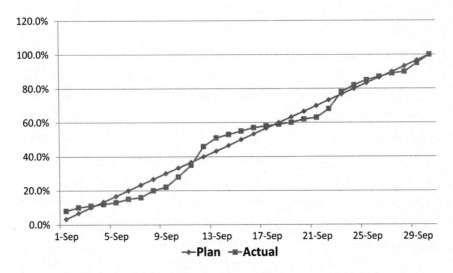

Figure 12.3 Daily Reporting of the Marketing SLA

direction, inefficiencies would occur. For example, if the Marketing team started off really slowly for the first three weeks and had a monster final week of the month to hit their lead quality goal, this created major issues for Sales. In this case, Sales would be sitting around twiddling their thumbs for the first three weeks of the month and then drown in lead flow during the final week.

Conversely, if the Marketing team crushed the first week's lead goal and then generated a slow trickle of leads for the rest of the month, the Sales team would be in a lot of trouble, even if Marketing successfully limped to their SLA goal. Sales wouldn't be able to keep up with the volume from the first weeks. Well-qualified leads would get lost simply because the team couldn't follow up quickly enough. Then, with lead flow drying up as the month progressed, salespeople would be left twiddling their thumbs. Having the actual lead value follow the ideal lead value as closely as possible represented critical execution, especially as the team grew.

In order to enforce the Sales SLA, we created a dashboard called the "Do Not Be on It" dashboard. This is a great example of "keeping it simple in Sales." This dashboard was simple. If a salesperson was on the dashboard, it meant the salesperson was violating the Sales SLA. For example, on the "Do Not Be on It" dashboard, we had a chart that showed any new leads that were not touched within one hour of converting through the website. We had a chart that showed any free trials that were one week old and had been called fewer than three times. We had a chart illustrating the demo requests that were three days old and had been touched fewer than two times. You get the point. Once you determine your Sales SLA, program these key measures into your "Do Not Be on It" dashboard and distribute it to the team daily.

"Send daily reports updating the entire Sales and Marketing team on the Sales and Marketing SLA. Manage the Sales and Marketing machine on a daily basis."

As you can see, this approach to Sales and Marketing alignment allowed Mike and me to run the business on a daily basis, rather than monthly or quarterly. By being precise with definitions, expectations, and quantified goals, both teams had a clear understanding of their respective missions and were accountable to one another. The Sales and Marketing machine was running smoothly.

To Recap

- The dysfunctional relationship between Sales and Marketing is the kiss of death in a buyer-driven world.
- Use the Sales and Marketing SLA to replace the subjective and qualitative aspects of the Sales/Marketing relationship with well-defined targets and quantified goals.
- The Marketing SLA provides a framework to put Marketing on a revenue quota, similar to Sales' dynamic.
- Sales is accountable to Marketing just like Marketing is accountable to Sales. The Sales SLA defines a series of behaviors expected of the Sales team to ensure each lead is worked effectively.
- Send daily reports updating the entire Sales and Marketing team on the Sales and Marketing SLA. Manage the Sales and Marketing machine on a daily basis.

PART V

Technology and Experimentation

13 | Technology to Sell Better, Faster

Over the last few decades, the business world has experienced technological advancements that have made it easier for Finance to manage its budgets, HR to manage its people, IT to manage its data, and even sales VPs to manage their forecasts.

However, how has technology helped the frontline salesperson? It really hasn't.

Most sales technology does not work for frontline salespeople. It creates work for salespeople. It creates admin tasks for salespeople. It takes salespeople off the phones. It takes salespeople away from selling.

Sales technology has been so ineffective for salespeople that many salespeople refuse to use it. Organizations suffer from sales technology

"Historically, sales technology has been built for the sales leader, not the salesperson. This technology does not work for salespeople. Instead, it creates work for salespeople."

adoption issues. As a result, the original value propositions for which the software is purchased, such as easy pipeline review or forecast analysis, become compromised due to incomplete or sloppily kept data.

How should companies respond to this issue? Should sales technology adoption be avoided altogether? Should companies simply let salespeople "do their thing"?

Absolutely not.

Technology represents an enormous opportunity for sales acceleration. Technology played a major role in my ability to accelerate sales at HubSpot. That said, to be effective, sales technology needs to be approached in the right way.

Modern sales technology enables two opportunities:

> "Companies should strive to adopt sales technology that enables better buying for customers and faster selling for salespeople."

1. *Sell faster:* Accelerate the current sales process by eliminating admin work and mundane tasks for salespeople.
2. *Sell better:* Create a better buying experience for customers by capturing buyer context and making that context available to salespeople wherever they are. As a result, salespeople can engage buyers with the most helpful information at the most helpful time.

In this chapter, I will provide detailed descriptions of how sales acceleration technology benefited our sales team at each stage of the sales process. As of the writing of this book, I had teamed up with one of our most talented product leaders at HubSpot, Christopher O'Donnell, to commercialize this sales acceleration technology so that every sales team could benefit from our insights. The first application that originated from these efforts was Sidekick, available for free at www.getsidekick.com.

Accelerate Lead Sourcing with Technology

One of the most time-consuming steps of the sales process is simply finding qualified buyers to call. I call this step "lead sourcing." Some organizations attempt to streamline the lead sourcing process by purchasing lists of supposedly "qualified leads." Unfortunately, these efforts typically yield a list of bad prospects, many of whom no longer even work at the companies listed.

Other organizations subscribe their salespeople to data sources, equipping their salespeople with the ability to filter through massive amounts of contacts to find the perfect prospect to call. Sadly, as the data often lacks accuracy and comprehensiveness, this filtering process becomes an extremely inefficient use of the salesperson's time.

When we at HubSpot set up our first team dedicated to sourcing leads and making proactive calls into the market, we made these same mistakes. After a number of frustrating cycles with purchased lists and data source subscriptions, this team ultimately resorted to simple searches in Google. These salespeople conducted Google searches for phrases that they presumed would yield a list of "good-fit" companies for the HubSpot service.

The process effectively yielded qualified companies on which to call. However, the time investment needed to source these companies was unsustainable. Here is how the process worked:

1. Conduct a Google search for a phrase that yields qualified companies for the HubSpot service.
2. Click through to the first company that looks interesting.
3. Scan the website to verify whether the company appears to be qualified for the HubSpot service.
4. If the company appears qualified, search for the company in our CRM to see if the company is already "owned" by another salesperson.
5. If the company is not already owned by another salesperson, conduct research online to find the key executives who would be involved in the purchase decision.

6. Conduct additional research to find the industry, revenue, territory, and contact information for the company and its executive contacts.
7. Type all of this information into the CRM.

Ten clicks. Ten minutes. One lead sourced.

That is a lot of admin work.

There had to be a better way. There had to be a way for technology to accelerate this lead sourcing process.

After some great work by our engineering team, we were able to evolve our lead sourcing process. Here's how it worked:

1. Conduct a Google search for a phrase that yields qualified companies for the HubSpot service.
2. Click through to the first company that looks interesting. All of the data necessary to evaluate the company appears in a browser sidebar next to the company website. With one click, the data can be added to the CRM.

The company summary, territory, revenue, key executives, existing CRM records, account ownership, and contact history are instantly available to the salesperson via a single click. As a bonus, at the bottom of the side panel is a list of companies similar to the company being evaluated. If our salesperson likes the lead she was viewing, the salesperson would probably like five similar ones as well. With one click, the salesperson could view the information on these additional companies and add these additional leads to the CRM.

Ten clicks. Ten minutes. Ten leads sourced!

Using the old process, it took a full business day to source 50 new leads. Using the Sidekick technology, sourcing 50 leads took less than one hour. That is sales acceleration! Less admin work. More time interacting with prospects. More time selling.

Sales technology can also create a better buying experience for customers throughout their buyer journey. Once a company is added as a lead in the CRM, the sales technology *enriches* the lead with useful context about the buyer. If that buyer had any prior engagement with our company, such as a visit to our website, an opening of one of our marketing emails, or a download of an ebook, that information would be automatically added to the lead. Any recent activity that the buyer had in social media would also be auto-

> *"Sales technology creates better buying experiences for customers by capturing customer context and making that context readily available to salespeople."*

matically added to the lead record. This contextual information provided guidance to our salespeople about the lead's specific interests. The salesperson would then be in a position to engage the buyer in a more helpful way.

Accelerate Sales Prospecting with Technology

Once the salesperson finds a list of companies to call, he attempts to connect with these companies, leaving a stream of voicemails and emails. Most organizations call this process "sales prospecting."

As salespeople begin their prospecting process, many of them sort their list of companies according to last activity date or, even worse, based on alphabetical order. As the salesperson leaves voicemails and/or sends emails, the only personalization in the message is the contact and company name. Aside from those basic details, every touch represents the same elevator pitch. You have probably been on the receiving end of plenty of these spam attempts. Have you ever found one compelling? Despite the market's resistance to this technique, it amazes me how many sales organizations take this approach.

Better salespeople layer in additional sophistication. Rather than simply calling their leads in alphabetical order or based on their last attempt date, they establish a strategic cadence based on the quality of the lead they are calling. These salespeople will also personalize their prospecting strategies much more effectively. They will check company news, such as a round of financing or an industry award, and reference tidbits of relevant information in their message.

While referencing company news may seem useful, is it really increasing the salesperson's ability to usher the company along its buyer journey? Wouldn't it be more useful for the salesperson to find out if someone from the company had visited the salesperson's website? If someone from the company had opened an email from the salesperson's marketing department? If someone from the company had opened an email from the salesperson? If someone from the company had mentioned your competitor in social media? Wouldn't it be helpful if a salesperson knew about these events as they were occurring? Wouldn't this information be more relevant than company news? Wouldn't this information help the salesperson engage with the buyer with the most helpful information at the most helpful time?

Yes!

We use technology to inform our salespeople when any of these events occur. As a result, our salespeople can engage immediately, referencing the specific interests of the buyer as demonstrated by their actions. Our salespeople should offer to help. This approach is useful to the buyer. This approach yields many more connects for the salesperson, accelerating the sales prospecting process.

The other aspect to sales prospecting is the accurate logging of activity. Failure to do so means no historical trail of engagement with each lead. It also means no evidence for the sales manager to see that the salesperson has actually been working. Unfortunately, traditional sales technology does not make logging activity easy. Below is a typical end-to-end prospecting process:

1. Click through to the first lead record to call.
2. Research company news that can be referenced in the voicemail and email.

3. Dial the number. Leave the voicemail.
4. Create a task in the CRM.
5. Categorize the task as a voicemail.
6. Save the voicemail task.
7. Compose an email.
8. Send the email.
9. Create a task in the CRM.
10. Categorize the task as an email send.
11. Copy and paste the email into the task.
12. Save the task.
13. Create a new task in the CRM to follow up in two days.
14. Save the task.

Remember, this process occurs every time the salesperson prospects to a potential buyer. This process might be conducted more than 50 times per day!

We used sales technology to automate this entire process. The salesperson should simply inform the sales technology once he is ready to prospect. From there, the system should cue up the first lead record to attempt. The system should show the entire context so the salesperson can quickly absorb it and get ready to engage in a helpful way. The system should dial the phone. If no connect occurs and the salesperson leaves a voicemail, the system should automatically log the voicemail. The system should suggest the follow-up email to send, personalize the email automatically, and log the email send in the CRM. The system should automatically schedule a task for the next follow-up according to the optimal cadence for that type of lead.

There is no call logging. There is no admin work. The system is working for the salesperson. The salesperson is 100 percent focused on what he does best: *selling*.

> *"Sales technology enables faster selling for salespeople by eliminating admin tasks and automating data capture."*

Accelerate Lead Engagement with Technology

Once traditional salespeople actually connect with their prospects, salespeople tend to force their prospects through their prefabricated sales process. Step-by-step, salespeople move the buyer through the process their sales manager established for them, often ignoring the needs and preferences of the buyer along the way. For each buyer, the same process is used. The same content is shared. The process is based on the salesperson's behavior and perception of the deal, not on the buyer's actions or needs. The salesperson tells their manager, "Yes, I gave them a demo." "Yes, I asked if they have budget."

This process yields a seemingly full pipeline of activity. However, much of the pipeline gets "stuck." The pipeline does not convert to customers or revenue. In reality, the pipeline quality is fabricated. It is not real.

During the lead engagement process, sales technology provides tools to assist buyers with their natural buying journey, not jam buyers through the salesperson's process. Ideally, the stages of a sales opportunity should not be driven by actions the salesperson takes but by the actions the buyer takes. Did the buyer confirm that the summary of the discovery call was accurate? Did the buyer open up the proposal? Did a VP- or C-level executive attend a product overview? Has someone in Finance reviewed the ROI study assembled by the salesperson? These actions are much better indicators of the status of an opportunity. In an ideal world, these buyer actions are captured by the sales technology. Opportunities are automatically moved forward and backward as buyer action or inaction is captured. This process eliminates the subjectivity or "gut feel" of a salesperson, which often contaminates the accuracy of a sales pipeline and forecast.

Aligning the opportunity stages with the buying journey also maximizes the likelihood that the sales team is in lockstep with the buyer along the way. Technology can assist the salesperson with this alignment. By truly understanding both the buyer persona (e.g., Small Business, Mid-Market, Enterprise) and the buyer's stage in their journey (e.g., Problem Definition, Solution Education, Solution Selection), technology can recommend the appropriate collateral to share with the buyer to help accelerate the process. If a salesperson is working with a mid-sized health care company investigating its compliance with a new FDA mandate, what is the most appropriate blog article or ebook or webinar that the salesperson's company has produced that would resonate with the prospect's specific buyer context? If a salesperson is working with an enterprise manufacturing company looking to support its distribution channel with a digital marketing budget, which case study would be most helpful for this buyer context? As companies accelerate their content production efforts, aligning sales collateral with buyer states represents a significant opportunity for technology to improve the sales process. This type of sales acceleration is beneficial to both the buyer and the seller.

Automated Reporting with Technology

These technology use cases have not only created better buying experiences for customers and shortened sales cycles for salespeople, but also automated the collection of critical data needed to manage the sales organization and the broader company. By implementing technology that actually helps the salesperson, adoption rises and, in turn, the integrity of the data becomes far more accurate.

Sales executives gain increased visibility into the answers to the following questions:

1. Is our pipeline positioned to achieve this quarter's target?
2. What are we forecasting for total revenue this quarter?
3. Is our "top of the funnel" activity on par with what will be needed to set us up for next quarter?

4. Where does each salesperson rank in total funnel activity (leads sourced, voicemails, connects, discovery calls, presentations, etc.) by day, by week, and by month?
5. How does a salesperson's current activity compare to her historic performance?
6. Is the sales team working with each newly generated lead in accordance with our Sales Service Level Agreement (SLA)?
7. Are there any leads, especially high-priority leads like demo requests or free trials, slipping through the cracks?

Marketers gain increased visibility into the answers to the following questions:

1. Are the leads I am producing being worked according to the Sales Service Level Agreement?
2. Which types of leads are accelerating through the buyer journey and which types are not?
3. Which salespeople are most effectively leveraging the collateral my team has made available?
4. Which collateral produces the highest level of prospect engagement? Are there particular slides or pages that are popular? Are there particular slides or pages that are ignored?
5. Is the sales team using the latest collateral?

Salespeople gain increased visibility into the answers to the following questions:

> *"Sales technology developed for the salesperson in the end benefits the sales manager with more accurate reporting to run the salesforce and the business."*

1. Which prospects have recently engaged with my sales emails and collateral?
2. How does my activity volume compare to the rest of the team?
3. Am I completing enough activity to achieve my overall goals?
4. Are any of my leads or opportunities falling through the cracks?

Most importantly, all of these parties have gained increased visibility without placing any additional burden on the salespeople. The data is accurate, and the data capture process is automated.

To Recap

- Historically, sales technology has been built for the sales leader, not the salesperson. This technology does not work for sales-people. Instead, it creates work for salespeople.
- Companies should strive to adopt sales technology that enables better buying for customers and faster selling for salespeople.
- Sales technology creates better buying experiences for customers by capturing customer context and making that context readily available to salespeople.
- Sales technology enables faster selling for salespeople by elim-inating admin tasks and automating data capture.
- Sales technology developed for the salesperson in the end benefits the sales manager with more accurate reporting to run the salesforce and the business.

---

14 | Running Successful Sales Experiments

Great teams have a core philosophy of continual improvement. Whether succeeding or failing, there is always a way to improve existing execution, adapt to changing market dynamics, or consider expansion into new areas. Maintaining a culture of experimentation is a great way to foster this philosophy of continual improvement.

Let's navigate back to year two of HubSpot's journey. We had had a great first year. We were fortunate to have Gail Goodman, CEO of ConstantContact, on our board of direc-tors. At the time, she pointed out, "Great year, but you guys are not experimenting enough. You have a very good model. It is working. But there must be ways to do it better. You are a young company. Try some things. Don't be afraid to fail."

I took those comments to heart, and now I can point to dozens of best

> *"Great teams have a core philosophy of continual improvement. A key ingredient to the sales acceleration formula is fostering a culture of experimentation."*

practices within the HubSpot sales organization that originated from Gail's philosophy. A key ingredient to the sales acceleration formula is fostering a culture of experimentation. I've included some of my favorite methods for establishing this environment.

Generating Ideas for Experiments

> *"A key role of the executive team is to set up a culture around innovation, rather than generate all of the big ideas themselves."*

At HubSpot, we had what I would call a "bottom-up" innovation funnel. Our most groundbreaking ideas didn't necessarily come from our executives or directors, but rather from our front line. They came from the employees who were talking with prospects, going head-to-head with the competition, and working with our customers on a daily basis. We hired really smart people. When smart people spend their days on the front line, they see the patterns, they innovate, and they come up with the ideas that can change the trajectory of the business.

Our job as an executive team was to create the environment in which this innovation process could occur. Our job was to incubate this innovation passion rather than come up with the big ideas ourselves. One technique we used was the internal "hackathon." Normally, these hackathons were focused on a specific problem that was relevant at the time, such as slow customer adoption of a new feature, a competitor's new offering, or an internal culture issue. A message was sent to the company, framing the problem and inviting anyone interested to participate in the hackathon to brainstorm solutions. Most of them occurred after hours. Often there was pizza and beer provided. Sometimes hundreds of people showed up. They were fun.

To kick off the hackathon, the organizer would frame the problem for the audience and set the agenda on how the brainstorming process would flow for the evening. Next, anyone who had an idea would pitch it to the audience for a minute or two. All ideas were recorded on a whiteboard. After approximately 30 minutes of idea generation, the crowd was polled to gauge interest in the various ideas on the board. The top 10 or so were selected and small breakout teams were formed around each idea. The teams spent about an hour discussing their assigned ideas and devising an experiment to test each concept. Once the plans were fully formed, each team circled back to present the details to the broader group.

If an idea was simple enough and required minimal investment, it would be executed by the individuals involved in the relevant business function. For the promising ideas that would require significant investment, the brainstorming groups would be invited to present the proposed experiment to the executive team at a dedicated experiment board meeting, where company leadership would decide whether to fund the experiment. If the idea was funded, it would be added to our innovation pipeline. The innovation pipeline was monitored each month and, when applicable, teams would deliver a status update to the experiment board on their particular projects. The board was there to provide guidance and decide whether to keep each experiment going, dedicate additional resources, or discontinue certain projects to make room for other innovations.

Another key element of the innovation culture was the transparency we had throughout the organization. A successful innovation culture requires all employees to feel like they are "CEO" of their functional area. To be CEO, they need a full picture of the happenings within their business. As such, all of the monthly financials were made available to every employee. They were reviewed at company meetings. They were posted on the company wiki. The tactical priorities of the overall business as well as those of each executive were published on the wiki and reviewed at company meetings. Monthly updates on progress against the operational plan were reported to the entire company. Customer happiness was measured through a monthly NPS survey. The raw data and summary from these reports were shared with the entire company. An employee NPS was conducted once per quarter. The raw data and summary from these surveys were shared with the entire company. The company wiki itself was extremely active. The executive team was often responding to questions and comments. It was a great way to leverage technology and flatten the steep communication pyramid often seen in more archaic organizations.

The final component of our innovation culture was the solidification of an "innovation" career track at the organization. I saw three basic career tracks that employees pursued at HubSpot. One track was the leadership track. Once functional expertise was established, these employees entered into leadership training and started to pursue management opportunities within their area of the organization. Another direction was the "functional expert" track. Perhaps the employee was a career salesperson that really wanted to grow as an individual contributor. Perhaps the employee was a career engineer that wanted to grow as a code ninja. We were proactive about establishing well-defined, attractive paths for people who shared these aspirations. The third approach was the "innovation" track. These employees were most passionate about breaking new ground. They were heavy participants in the hackathons, wiki threads, and other innovation programs. Many of them were eventually selected to lead an experiment. Most importantly, if and when they succeeded, they established a new trajectory for their career at HubSpot. Being able to point to successful leaders in the organization who had achieved their positions via the innovation track was key to our culture's credibility.

Best Practices of Experiment Execution

As the sales team grew to a sizeable level, it was not unusual for me to have several experiments running at any given time. We ran experiments on new demand generation tactics, potential addressable markets, sales methodologies, and new products. The vibrant Hub-Spot partner program, our aggressive international expansion, and revisions to our selling methodology all originated from our experimentation framework.

Why make a major change without first testing it on a smaller scale?

Over the years, we played close attention to the generic process required to execute a successful experiment. The process is as follows:

1. *Define a clear goal and measure of success:* This sounds obvious, but you would be surprised how often this step is overlooked during experiment setup. Three weeks in, the team is "in the weeds" of the experiment, failing to see the big picture, and losing sight of the original intention of the initiative. Equally as frustrating, they reach the end of the experiment, generate a set of results, and there is no consensus around whether the results indicate success. Set a clear objective. Think of it as a thesis for the experiment. Define what success and failure look like. Be absolutely disciplined about finding a way to quantify that success.

   "Follow a specific formula for experiment execution so that you can be confident your experiments are efficient and effective."

2. *Design the experiment execution:* Determine a way to test the experiment thesis in the least amount of time with the least amount of investment. The time and investment necessary is an important factor in determining the attractiveness of the experiment. Imagine a potential experiment that could be run in a day for less than $100, and if successful, could triple your business. You would run that experiment in a heartbeat. However, if the experiment would take a year to test and cost hundreds of thousands of dollars, it would be far less attractive. The potential return would need to be extraordinarily high to even consider running it. Finding the lowest-cost, shortest path to experimentation is critical.

3. *Choose a leader:* Ideally, the experiment evolved from one of the company innovation processes and the employee who thought it up has the skills, the passion, and the time to lead the experiment. If so, the individual's personal attachment to the initiative will generate exponentially higher motivation and drive to succeed than if the experiment was inherited from someone else. Great experiment leaders have passion for the idea, knowledge about the functional areas being tested, and professional goals that the experiment will help them achieve.

4. *Assemble the team:* Most experiments require a team to run, especially in sales. I strongly urge you to assign at least two people to every experiment. I also recommend you choose top performers, rather than average performers, to be part of the experiment. What I am looking for in the first experiment phase is a "true negative." If I put two top sales performers on the experiment and the experiment fails, there is a high probability that the idea wasn't feasible. If two of our top people could not pull it off, how could we roll this out to the broader team? On the other hand, if I put one average salesperson on the experiment and I don't see promising results, I haven't necessarily learned anything. Did the experiment fail because I had the wrong person involved or did it fail because it was not a feasible idea? Execute the first phase of the experiment with multiple top performers and look for "true negatives."

5. *Establish routine check-ins:* Set expectations on how often the company will evaluate the progress of the experiments. We held a monthly experiment meeting with senior leadership to review data. The experiment leader, along with her team, would have 30 minutes to present their progress and address questions from the executive team. If progress was weak, there might be a decision made to discontinue funding. If success was apparent, there might be additional funding allocated or expansion plans discussed.

To Recap

- Great teams have a core philosophy of continual improvement. A key ingredient to the sales acceleration formula is fostering a culture of experimentation.
- A key role of the executive team is to set up a culture around innovation, rather than generate all of the big ideas themselves.
- Follow a specific formula for experiment execution so that you can be confident your experiments are efficient and effective.

15

HubSpot's Most Successful Sales Experiments

In an attempt to illustrate the impact of sales experiments, let me walk through two very successful examples we ran at HubSpot. One example is a go-to-market experiment. The other is a sales methodology experiment.

The HubSpot Value Added Reseller (VAR) Program

In the fall of 2007, I hired Pete Caputa as HubSpot's fourth salesperson. Like me, Pete was a nontraditional sales hire. He was an engineer by training. He was coming from a small startup, where he'd been CEO. He had some solid sales training under his belt.

Only a few months into the job, Pete became extraordinarily passionate about starting a VAR program. Up to that point, we had been acquiring 100 percent of our business through a direct sales model, calling on the inbound leads from our website and converting them into customers. Pete envisioned a new sales channel. He wanted to focus on all of the small marketing agencies, web design shops, and SEO consultants that were following the HubSpot story. He believed we could convince these organizations to resell our software.

Prior to Pete's arrival, we had considered a VAR program. In fact, we had even experimented with the program with a large reseller. I find that most start-ups consider selling through resellers as an attractive starting point. Rather than invest in the hiring and management of a large direct sales force, wouldn't it be great to just get someone else to do it for you?

For most early start-ups, this approach fails. We were fortunate to have executives from many successful software-as-a-service (SaaS) businesses on the HubSpot advisory board. They advised us against starting a VAR program in the early phases of the company. They warned that these partnerships required significant effort to establish, especially with resellers of reasonable scale. Furthermore, getting an agreement in place is only half the battle. You still need to capture the mindshare of the partner's sales team. The sales team needs to be trained on your product. Oftentimes, your product is lost in the shuffle of dozens or even hundreds of other products they are expected to resell.

The other major issue with a partner strategy is the lack of a feedback cycle from the partner's front line to your product team and executives. It is rare that a start-up nails its product-market fit right out of the gate. As a start-up initially develops its own sales muscle, the most valuable outputs of that muscle are not necessarily the early customers and revenue that is generated. Instead, the most valuable output is the learnings from the prospective buyers. The more effective the team is at understanding the needs and preferences of its addressable market and communicating that information back to the company to iterate on the product, pricing, and packaging, the more likely the start-up is to achieve product-market fit and accelerate. When sales is run through an outside partner channel, a lot of that feedback is lost. Often these partner salespeople are not physically or emotionally connected to your company. They have little incentive to capture feedback from prospective buyers and communicate it back to the team.

I agreed wholeheartedly with this insight and appreciated the advice from our advisors, but Pete was both passionate and persistent about starting a partner program at HubSpot. Furthermore, there was our desire to foster an "innovation" culture where great ideas from our smart employees were valued and evaluated. I told Pete that if he hit 120 percent of his quarterly goal, he could start experimenting with VAR.

Needless to say, Pete did it.

The next quarter, we set up the experiment. We agreed that Pete would continue to be held responsible for his quota responsibilities, but we would give him a bit of funding for the VAR experiment, which he would run as a nights and weekends effort. The goal of the experiment was to explore whether we could leverage VARs to acquire new customers at an attractive cost and who would be successful using the HubSpot software. Success of the experiment was defined as five new customers acquired through one or more VARs. All five customers needed to have the HubSpot software set up and log in to the platform at least once per week for the first month.

Pete did it again.

The next quarter, we made the VAR program Pete's full-time job. We gave him a marketing budget and set him off with a new set of goals. He hit the next set of goals. We increased the marketing budget and gave him budget to hire two dedicated salespeople. The program was ready to scale.

As time progressed, we measured his VAR channel just like the rest of the business. For you SaaS experts out there, we measured LTV/CAC, payback period, salesperson productivity, customer retention, and a few other metrics. The results were phenomenal.

Six years later, Pete oversaw a VAR-focused team of 100 cross-functional employees and was responsible for a significant amount of HubSpot's monthly new revenue generation.

Imagine if we had never given Pete that shot. The VAR experiment is an amazing example of a simple, contained, and relatively cheap bet with the potential for enormous gains. Fortunately, in our case, those gains were realized.

GPCT

As I mentioned in Chapter 5, the first qualifying matrix we used at HubSpot was BANT (Budget, Authority, Need, Timing). As we reviewed sales opportunity after sales opportunity, it became apparent that, in our context, the "N" in BANT ("Need") had become the most important component of the discovery process. HubSpot salespeople who established a strong "Need" with their prospective buyers had very high lead-to-customer conversion rates.

A well-developed "Need" sounded like this: "The buyer is adding two salespeople in Q4 and needs to increase lead flow by 20 percent by the start of the quarter in order to support the sales expansion. If they do not increase lead flow, the new salespeople will need to resort to cold calling, which has been unsuccessful for the team in the past. The expanded sales team will likely fail at accelerating customer acquisition if the company does not increase lead flow proportionately."

Some of our salespeople did not develop "Need" well. These salespeople had much lower lead-to-customer conversion rates. They failed to understand their prospects' needs beyond the surface level. When I would ask these salespeople about the needs they had uncovered, they responded generically, "The buyer needs more leads, just like everyone else." No kidding! Why? How many? How did they come up with that number? What happens if they do not generate more leads? Where does increasing lead flow fit on their overall priority list? If our salespeople didn't have these answers, it was a bad sign.

A few years into the business, we were struggling to develop effective "Need" discovery with some of our salespeople. A different approach was necessary. As a sales leadership team, we started the brainstorming process. Ultimately, we decided to iterate on our qualifying matrix. We came up with an improved matrix that better summarized the discovery approach our most successful salespeople were taking with potential buyers. We called this qualifying matrix GPCT (Goal, Plan, Challenges, Timeline).

Here are the details:

1. *Goal:* The business goals around which the prospect's company is rallying. As my mentor John McMahon once eloquently stated, "A well-developed goal is quantified and implicated." "Quantified" means there is a number attached to the goal (i.e., the prospective buyer needs to increase lead flow by 20 percent). "Implicated" means we understand the implication if the buyer does not achieve the goal (i.e., if the buyer does not increase lead flow by 20 percent, the buyer will have new salespeople with no leads to call; the buyer will essentially be spreading the same potential revenue across a larger sales team; salesperson productivity will decrease, and the buyer will likely fail to grow the business). The "Goal" helped us understand how much impact we could have with the buyer and gauge how important goal achievement would be to the buyer.

2. *Plan:* The business plan put in place to achieve the goal. In the HubSpot context, the "Goal" was typically oriented around lead generation. The "Plan" was, in turn, a marketing strategy meant to increase lead flow. Will the company increase its presence at trade shows? Will the company launch a direct mail campaign? Will the company increase its advertising spend, start a blog, ramp up cold calling, etc.? Uncovering the buyer's "Plan" helped us to assess whether we felt it was realistic and whether we could help. Ideally, our salespeople would identify a plan that would work and with which we could help (i.e., develop an inbound marketing program). We would obviously convert many of these sales

opportunities into customers. In contrast, we often found buyers with plans that, in our experience, were likely to fail. A common example of this scenario was a company that planned to purchase a list of cold prospects and cold email them. Not only did this strategy yield few leads, but also the cold emailing activity increased the likelihood that the company's email would be sent directly to spam folders, negatively impacting future sales and marketing efforts. In this case, we needed to educate the buyer's team on the dangers of their current plan and redirect them toward a more effective strategy. These were tougher sales opportunities to navigate. In reality, customers could actually execute their cold emailing plan using the HubSpot software, but allowing them to purchase on those grounds would simply lead to a failed campaign and a bad customer experience. It was better for the customer if we educated them on the dangers of their strategy and redirected them toward a more successful approach.

3. *Challenges:* The challenges associated with implementing the buyer's plan. Does the company have the right staff in place to execute the plan? Does the company have the budget necessary to execute the plan? Are there gaps in software functionality and vendor capabilities that will hurt the plan? Understanding the prospective buyer's challenges enabled us to understand how we could most effectively help. If we genuinely felt we could help overcome the challenges, all parties would be comfortable moving forward. If there were challenges remaining that we couldn't address directly, we could at least help find alternative solutions in the spirit of the relationship.

4. *Timeline:* The date by which the prospective buyer needs to achieve the goal. How did the buyer come up with that date? What are the consequences of not achieving the goal by that date? How can HubSpot's solution help accelerate goal achievement, and how can we communicate that effectively to the buyer?

The more the HubSpot sales leadership team discussed the GPCT qualifying matrix, the more we liked it. We tested the new matrix against a number of sales opportunities and found that it provided a much better guide for the salespeople to navigate the buyer journey.

Most companies would roll out a change like this at their annual sales meeting. "Let me introduce our new sales qualifying matrix. GPCT!" At the sales meeting, the sales team would be exposed to the definition of GPCT. They would learn how it could be applied to their opportunity pipeline. They would likely attend a few hours of classroom-style training to integrate it into their current process. Six months later, 20 percent of the team would still be using GPCT. The rest of the team would have settled back into their old ways.

We took a different approach. Instead of announcing GPCT to the entire team, we set up an experiment.

The goal of the experiment was to understand whether transitioning from BANT to GPCT would improve the discovery stage of our sales process and, in turn, increase lead-to-customer conversion rates, salesperson productivity, and customer success. In the first phase of the experiment, we planned to teach GPCT to our five top salespeople. Success was defined as a 10 percent increase in lead-to-customer conversion rates, salesperson productivity, and customer success within six months.

As I mentioned, the phase one team consisted of our five top salespeople. The team leader was Andrew Quinn, who at the time was our head of sales training and the best coach in the company. It was purposely a team of rock stars. The objective of the first phase was to find a *true negative*. If this star-studded team, led by our best coach, could not improve its performance with GPCT, then it was likely a bad idea to roll the new model out to the entire team. However, if GPCT did work, it would be worth a shot to see if similar improvements could be realized with the next tier of salespeople.

For six months under Andrew's leadership, this team gathered a few evenings per week to discuss GPCT. The team watched film of one another using GPCT on live discovery calls. They reviewed their opportunity pipelines through the GPCT lens. They established clear guidelines on how to define the key elements of each stage of the matrix. They established the best questions to uncover GPCT with each prospect.

Not surprisingly, Andrew and the phase one team crushed the success metrics we established for them. Furthermore, an additional, unanticipated positive outcome was realized. Adoption of GPCT by the broader team had begun organically. The phase one salespeople happened to be physically spread throughout the inside sales floor. Their neighbors could, of course, overhear the qualifying calls they were having with prospective buyers. They started to ask the top performers about this new model. Word started to spread across the floor about GPCT, the evening sessions, and the phase one team's initial success. Other salespeople started to ask the top performers to help them adopt the GPCT approach. It was beautiful! By the time we were ready to announce GPCT to the entire sales team, everyone had heard of the new strategy, and 80 percent of the sales floor has already bought in and were using it.

What a stark contrast to the traditional "annual kickoff" rollout. This *experimental* approach yielded two positive outcomes. First, the experimental approach provided us with a safe, low-risk way for us to test the value of the GPCT framework. Second, the experimental approach enabled us to gain buy-in across the floor in a more efficient way than the traditional annual sales kickoff would have achieved.

The VAR program and GPCT are just two examples of many successful experiments at HubSpot. An even greater number of failed experiments existed as well. The HubSpot culture of innovation and disciplined experiment execution empowered employees to constantly challenge the norm, enabled us to fail without causing operational catastrophes, and incubated some of the most important strategic shifts that propelled the company to the next level.

16 | Conclusion: Where Do We Go from Here?

There are three layers of takeaways from this book.

At the surface layer, I hope this book has presented you with some useful tactics around building a sales team in a scalable, predictable way. I hope that my anecdotes provide a blueprint for how you can effectively hire, train, and manage a high-performing sales team. I hope that you appreciate the power of executing an inbound selling model and empowering your organization with a culture of experimentation. I hope, too, that you understand the competitive advantage that can be unleashed for your business with the proper adoption of sales technology, benefiting both your salespeople and your customers.

Beneath the surface, I hope this book has inspired you to challenge the norm as you scale sales. I prefaced almost every anecdote with a word of caution that the tactics discussed worked in our context, but may not work in yours. Constantly seek out the latest, best practices; study the sales strategies of the most successful companies. However, appreciate how your buyer context is special. Only apply the strategies that are relevant to your team and product. Challenge the norm in the areas in which you are unique. Innovate. Share your learnings. Contribute to the field of sales.

That leads us to the final layer. At its core, I have an aspirational hope and dream that this book contributes to a foundation of new sales philosophies that fundamentally change the sales field. An evolution such as this has not happened in quite some time, and it is much needed. Let me explain.

For decades, thought leaders in both academia and the business community have cast doubt on the notion that sales and sales leadership skills can be taught. It is difficult—almost impossible—to find a major in sales. And yet, effective sales execution is arguably one of the most important drivers of company success. Despite the current lack of formal training programs, I am optimistic about the future. In the past year, I have been approached by at least a dozen leaders in the academic and business communities looking to challenge the status quo and assemble a formal curriculum in sales. I hope more influencers embrace these efforts in the years to come.

The best and brightest students graduating from top universities have, for many years, pursued rewarding careers as investment bankers, management consultants, engineers, entrepreneurs, lawyers, and doctors. Traditionally, they have delegated the sales jobs to their less-accomplished peers. However, I am confident that this will change. In the last few years, I have seen a renewed interest in sales by top students from the world's best universities. These students see that many Fortune 500 CEOs' careers started in sales and appreciate the importance of sales in almost every aspect of entrepreneurial success. They understand the financial rewards of a high-performing career in sales.

Over the years, buyers have migrated from reluctantly engaging with salespeople to proactively avoiding them. Salespeople are notoriously regarded as manipulative, deceitful, and borderline unethical. It is these perceptions, and the behaviors that create them, that will lead to the continued degradation of the sales profession. We need to embrace the early incubation of modern sales tactics in order to change this stigma. Salespeople should be thought of as helpful advisors and respected thought leaders. They should be sought after in times of crisis, just as doctors are, and their diagnoses should be taken seriously.

As both buyers and sellers, we should all want this evolution for the sales field. We need to accelerate the journey toward this vision; however, I don't know how. This is where I need your help.

Somebody out there holds the most important element of the sales acceleration formula: improving the underlying global perception of sales itself.

Perhaps it is you.

All of the Proceeds of This Book Will Be Donated to BUILD-Boston

BUILD, founded in 1999, is an innovative college preparatory program, whose mission is to use entrepreneurship to excite and propel disengaged, low-income high school students to college and career success. In BUILD, students develop their own business ideas, write business plans, pitch to investors, and launch real businesses. This real-world business experience makes school relevant and motivates disengaged youth to succeed. To help them become college-eligible, students also receive tutoring, test prep, mentoring, and advising for their schoolwork and college planning. At BUILD, entrepreneurship is the hook—but college is the goal. Over the past 13 years, 95 percent of BUILD seniors have been accepted to college, with more than 80 percent accepted to four-year colleges and universities. For more information, visit: www.build.org.

Index